THE SEASON OF BIRDS AND STONES

CRUX
THE GEORGIA SERIES IN
LITERARY NONFICTION

The Season of Birds and Stones

ESSAYS

Yelizaveta P. Renfro

University of Georgia Press • Athens

Published by the University of Georgia Press
Athens, Georgia 30602
www.ugapress.org

Designed by Melissa Buchanan
Set in Arno Pro
Printed and bound by Integrated Books International
The paper in this book meets the guidelines for permanence and durability of the Committee on Production Guidelines for Book Longevity of the Council on Library Resources.

Printed in the United States of America
30 29 28 27 26 P 5 4 3 2 1

EU Authorized Representative
Easy Access System Europe—Mustamäe tee 50, 10621 Tallinn, Estonia,
gpsr.requests@easproject.com

Library of Congress Control Number: 2026931848
ISBN (paperback): 9780820377308
ISBN (epub): 9780820377315
ISBN (PDF): 9780820377322

For Nick

CONTENTS

THE SEASON OF BIRDS AND STONES

Denali National Park and Preserve

THE TWENTIETH BEAR

Denali National Park and Preserve, Alaska
July 2015

"She's out today," James says. We catch our first glimpse, at mile 9—Denali, the great one. So that's it, I think. The tallest mountain in North America: austere and remote and imposing—yes, all of these things, just like a postcard image. Now I've seen it with my own eyes, but I am too dazed and jet-lagged to muster a deep reaction. Is there a box to mark somewhere? Tallest mountain, check.

I've spent two nights at James's house in Fairbanks, where I've moved in a fog of discombobulation, marveling at the proliferation of pale-trunked trees, which remind me of Russia, and forgetting to sleep at night, another reminder of Russia—the white nights of a Saint Petersburg summer. "Tell me what time it is without looking at your watch," James said to me on my first evening. "Eight o'clock," I guessed, and then when I checked my wrist, I discovered it was nearing midnight, the sapphire gloaming in the sky throwing off my sense of time. I've been mildly addled since, going through the motions of grocery shopping for my wilderness adventure, filling my cart haphazardly with canned meats and ramen and instant oatmeal and apples. How much can I eat in ten days? The question perplexes me, and I buy too much.

But now, driving down the park road, something new: We come to a checkpoint at mile 15, beyond which the pavement gives way to gravel and private cars are not normally permitted. Since we're in James's Subaru Impreza, we are required to present documentation and explanation to the ranger in the booth: I'm the artist-in-residence headed to Toklat cabin at mile 53, and James is giving me a ride. We have special permission to drive on the park road. After questioning and document checks, we're allowed through, and as the miles unspool, I begin to grow numbly inured to the landscape: Spectacular vistas flash past with mountain, tundra, braided rivers, fireweed, all the Alaska things, and occasionally we pass green or tan buses disgorging tourists with cameras at rest stops.

At last, in the early afternoon, we arrive at my cabin at Toklat, where we unload. With a long drive back to Fairbanks ahead of him, James soon departs, and I'm left wandering around my cabin, looking at the two-inch nails, protruding sharp end out, that stud the shutters—which I should keep closed when I am away to deter curious animals from visiting. And when I say *animals* I think *bears.* I don't know what to make of all this, being left here, in the middle of official *wilderness,* when barely five days ago I was checking my email and Facebook in my suburban New England house. My arrival here was preceded by months of planning, saving money, orchestrating childcare schedules. To come here I have left behind my husband and two children, ages seven and ten. I have given up the opportunity to teach a summer class. I have put my life on hold to enter the wilderness.

And yet the term *wilderness* seems like a misnomer. Though my cabin sits smack dab in the middle of officially designated Wilderness (with a capital W), I can see the gravel park road from my front porch. The Toklat River Contact Station, housed in an enormous tent and staffed during the day by rangers and Alaska Geographic bookstore employees, is perhaps a quarter of a mile down the road. I can easily catch a bus there to travel to other parts of the park. And a half a mile north of the tent is Toklat road camp, the temporary summer home of about thirty people, the rangers and road crew that serve the western end of the park. Running, I could reach people within minutes, if necessary. But standing outside my cabin in the bright silence of the evening, I am alone. I don't know what to make of the brief, flaring fairy tale summer that burns itself out in an exuberance of light, the fireweed that blooms up its stalk, marking the progression of the short season, the absence of snakes and ticks—the critters I'm used to watching for—but an abundance of bears and moose, where tree line is at a paltry 3,000 feet or below, and where, I am told, some of the plants of the lower forty-eight can be found blossoming in miniature in the tundra beneath my feet.

When a friend who hails entirely from big cities asked me, Wouldn't I be afraid to be alone in the Alaska wilderness, where I might *get eaten by a bear?*, I said with bravado that I found it scarier to walk the streets of New York City surrounded by that terrible press of people, that I found big city life scarier than wilderness, and I still believe that, and I am still mostly unafraid of bears, but that's not to say that I walk with confidence in the night to my outhouse, which is located about fifty feet up a slope among trees. But I also don't carry the can of bear spray that I was issued during my orientation; the outhouse doesn't seem far enough away to necessitate arming myself, and I don't want to be that clumsy shrinking violet who loses the bear spray down the outhouse hole in the dark on her first night alone, which seems a far more likely outcome than a bear encounter.

The bears begin on the morning of day 2. I'm on a westbound shuttle bus, heading deeper into the park, nearing the Eielson Visitor Center at mile 66, when a voice from the front cries "Bear!" The bus comes to a sudden stop, and every head and telephoto camera lens swivels to the left, fixating on the same point a couple hundred yards away.

"It's probably a male," our gravelly voiced driver Mike says over the bus's speakers. I watch the distant bear shape traversing the landscape, walking on a sand bar above a braided river. The bus fills with the murmur of voices and the constant firing of cameras; those seated on the far side stand in the aisle and lean over the heads of those on the bear side of the bus. "Well, this is an interesting development," says Mike. I scan the landscape and spot a lone caribou walking in the riverbed. The animals are approaching one another, the bear from the west above the river and the caribou from the east in the riverbed. We watch the drama unfold. "Probably nothing will happen," Mike croons. "This time of year the bears are well-fed and lazy." The bus grows silent in anticipation as the two animals near one another. The caribou plods on at a steady pace, apparently unconcerned about the bear, but the bear stops and turns its head to watch the caribou. For nearly an entire minute, the bear watches the progress of the caribou as it approaches, passes within about fifty yards, and then moves away. Finally, the bear resumes course, continuing east above the river. The camera clicks and chirps gradually die down; Mike puts the bus back into drive, and we continue on our journey to Eielson.

I watch the passengers settle into their seats; some scroll through photos on their screens. "Well, we've seen it," says a white-haired woman to the graying man beside her. "We got our bear." They are sitting directly ahead of me. I watch them turn to look at the mountain as we approach Eielson. She's out again, and the view here—thirty-three miles from the peak—is astonishing. Like a coy beauty, the mountain shrouds herself in clouds every two out of three days in summer, so a clear day is a prize. The woman leans contentedly on the man's shoulder: They've bagged both in one day, the mountain and a bear.

At Eielson, most of the tourists stick close to the visitor center, some of them venturing out to do the Tundra Loop Trail, an easy one-third-mile walk. But after being on the bus, I want to go further, to step into the landscape, to stop viewing it like a film that unspools its footage in a bus window. I decide to hike up to the ridge and over the other side to get a glimpse of Denali away from the park road. Denali has very few trails—most are under two miles and are near the main entrance—in order to preserve the character of a trailless wilderness. Visitors are encouraged to hike off-trail across the tundra, but few do. Today, I am one of those few. As I walk across the springy tundra, a thought sticks in my mind: I might encounter a bear. And I suspect that seeing a bear out here, outside of the safety of a bus, away from people, would be a different experience altogether.

Day 3 in Denali: I'm hoping for bears. I'm not actively looking for them—that seems foolhardy—but I'll be glad if a bear crosses my path: safely, at the appropriate three-football-fields remove, or from the refuge of a bus.

This time I'm on an eastbound bus, backtracking out of the park over the miles that I covered that first day with James when I was still in such a daze that my eyes passed, almost unseeing, over landscape.

The truth is, I've come here to watch people watching wilderness as much as I've come to watch the wilderness, and this is why I like to spend my time riding buses with tourists. Many of the visitors are visibly older than I am—and I am forty. I learned during my orientation that the average age of a Denali visitor is around sixty. Many have saved for years to make this trip of a lifetime—the one time they will get to see Alaska. For some, due to itineraries that pack in every possible Alaska attraction, today is the one day in their entire lives that they will spend in Denali. In comparison, my ten days seem like an extravagance—but even I will glimpse only a tiny sliver of a single Denali season.

Going over Polychrome Pass—famous for its hairpin turns and sheer drops—I see bear no. 5. In the distant braided river below, its channels of water glinting like veins of precious metal in the morning sunlight, the bear stands as still as a statue, as if posing in the landscape. The bus stops; the cameras begin to go off. For a moment, I am frozen, just looking. This, I realize, is the bear I will think of when people say *Did you see any bears in Alaska?* Yes, I saw this bear—this still creature that seems to have stopped on a sandbar in order to become part of my ideal photograph. *Bear of the Braided River,* I have titled it, even before I have taken out my camera to capture a single shot.

Immediately, we encounter another bear—so blond it looks white against tundra—and shortly thereafter, we hit the real bear jackpot: Just fifty feet from the park road, a blonde sow noses at bushes while her two chocolate-colored cubs gambol and wrestle. The stutter and bleeping of cameras fill the bus, and soon, other buses line up to get a view. As we watch the cavorting cubs, our driver, Mona, tells us bear facts: that the cubs are often born dark and grow lighter in color as they mature, that the brown bears of Denali have an 85 percent vegetarian diet and are not as large as salmon-fed bears, that the bears are so habituated to buses that we are, for all intents and purposes, inside a giant photographer's blind. "We've been incredibly lucky today," she says. And we have. By the time we reach the park entrance, we've seen a total of six bears, averaging more than one per ten miles of park road. Some unlucky visitors can spend a dozen hours on the bus, taking the road to the end and back, and never glimpse a single bear.

Day 4. I'm waiting for my daily bear. And I have confirmed with park visitors: They, too, are here to see bears. And they want to know all about my bears: how many I've seen, and under what circumstances. We want each other's stories, but so far, my stories are just affirmations: *Yup, I've seen bears. Out of bus windows. They were walking or digging or sleeping or eating or smacking their cubs or just standing there. They were being bears. Nothing happened.*

I know the park wildlife rules by heart: the twenty-five yards of space that moose, wolves, and caribou require, the three hundred yards to give a bear. I know the protocol for what to do if I encounter a bear. First, try not to encounter bears. Avoid them. Scan the landscape. Shout "Hello, Mr. Bear!" at willow thickets and over ridges and in areas with poor visibility. If you see a bear at a distance, reroute. Give it a wide berth: three football fields. That's a comfortable distance from a bear. If you come upon a bear unexpectedly and the bear sees you, don't run. Raise your hands in the air to look big and talk to the bear. "Look here, Mr. Bear, I'm a human being, and you're a bear, so we have no business to conduct together. I'm just going to slowly move away while you go about your berry eating. You have to meet your two-hundred-thousand-berry daily quota, which means you have no time for dillydallying." The bear may have no interest in you and do nothing. Or the bear may false-charge you: running at you and then veering away at the last instant. Stand your ground. Keep looking big. If you have bear spray, you can shoot a charging bear when it's about twenty-five feet away, and then again when it gets closer. Aim for the nose. A can of spray lasts seven seconds, so plan accordingly.

During my orientation on my first day, Ranger Cass told me not to be fearful. "There isn't a bear in this park that knows you're food, and there isn't a bear in this park that knows your backpack has food," he said. "So go out there. Be brave."

But he also told me about the man who was eaten by a bear here in 2012: the first time in the park's history. He told me all the things the man had done wrong. Since that time, I've heard the story from three other rangers and a bus driver. They tell it as a cautionary tale: How Not to Act Around Bears.

The man, forty-nine-year-old Richard White, left a partial record of what happened in the twenty-six photos that were later found on his camera. He had come far too close to a foraging bear—between forty and sixty yards—and he photographed the bear for nearly eight minutes. In the final images, the bear has turned its attention on White and is moving in his direction. According to a news report, the bear seemed "agitated" and had "a definite, focused stare."

After the killing, the bear secured White's body in a food cache. Several hours later, three hikers found the man's backpack and bloodied clothing and summoned rangers. Eventually, the bear—a six-hundred-pound mature boar, about five years old—was found and killed. The attack occurred near the Toklat River about three miles south of the park road—and three miles south of my cabin.

It's not just bears that are on my mind. On a hike on the Eielson Alpine Trail up Thorofare Ridge, I encounter an arctic ground squirrel coming out of a hole. It stands up on its hind legs, twitching its nose as if analyzing a scent. We are just ten feet apart, and the animal's eyes seem to be on me. Perhaps a foot long, stout and black-eyed, it faces me straight on, and we watch each other. Then with a flash of its white-speckled back, it's gone. But I stand there for a minute, hoping it will reemerge. I've heard about arctic ground squirrels from park rangers and bus drivers, but now that I've actually seen one with my own eyes, I am smitten.

Most visitors are after charismatic megafauna—bears, wolves, moose, caribou, Dall sheep—but I'm equally enchanted by the squirrels. They're nothing like the tree-dwelling eastern gray squirrels I see daily in Connecticut. These beefy, stumpy-tailed northern cousins have white-speckled beige coats and live in mazes of underground burrows in areas of arctic tundra with good drainage. They can grow to a length of almost twenty inches, and the males can weigh more than three pounds. Active only about three or four months during summer, the squirrels hibernate for up to three-quarters of the year. I've learned all of this from rangers and bus drivers, but now I'm doing additional research over the spotty internet connection at road camp to learn more about these elusive creatures I've just barely caught sight of.

If hibernation were an extreme sport, the arctic ground squirrel would be the world champion. A *Scientific American* article explains how, in the 1980s, researchers at the University of Alaska Fairbanks implanted temperature-sensitive radio transmitters in the abdomens of a dozen ground squirrels then left them in outdoor wire cages to hibernate. The animals' body temperatures dropped to -2.9°C, the lowest ever recorded in living mammals. And yet, due to a process known as "supercooling," their blood doesn't freeze solid, but remains liquid. Because the squirrels are beyond sleep when their body temperatures are this low, they shiver and shake themselves every couple of weeks until they reach normal body temperatures for a period of twelve to fifteen hours so that they can preserve vital neural connections. Then they plunge back into torpor.

Walking back to my cabin from road camp, I spot a golden eagle carrying off an arctic ground squirrel in its talons. I keep standing there, looking at the empty sky, long after the bird has flown out of sight.

I'm in the Toklat Ranger Contact Station—the tent—talking to Ranger Bob and Ranger Tina, gregarious husband-and-wife ranger team and erstwhile schoolteachers from Tennessee. In the lull between buses, we have the place to ourselves.

Ranger Bob wanders to the tent entrance—perhaps to look for approaching buses on the park road—while Tina and I keep talking.

"Bear!" Bob suddenly calls.

Tina and I move to the tent entrance and step outside with Bob, who is looking south toward the road. We follow his gaze and see a bear nosing around in the willows near the river, perhaps fifty yards away. For a moment, we all just watch.

I am acutely aware that I am standing on the ground, on my two legs; I am no longer up high, ensconced in metal and glass, inside a vessel that can move faster than a bear. Suddenly, this is no longer a wild animal park safari. The bear and I are both just animals out here in the wide world, and our paths just might cross. The bear has claws, teeth, five hundred pounds of bulk. I have my much-smaller physique, my wits, a can of bear spray in my pack. And today, at least, I have two park rangers.

Bob and Tina watch the bear as it wanders through the vegetation. Because as rangers their first priority is to keep visitors safe, they tell me that if the bear comes closer, I should step inside the tent and shut the door behind me—though the thick canvas walls don't offer sound protection. But the bear is moving away from us, down into the riverbed and out of view. We know it's still there only because a couple of buses coming from the east stop on the bridge for the passengers to take pictures. When the buses eventually roll into Toklat, Bob keeps the passengers contained to the northern end of the parking area, instructing them to use the vault toilets furthest from the tent. Then the bear comes back into view, walking out of the riverbed and heading west over a rise, in the approximate direction of my cabin, where it disappears.

"We'll drive you home," Bob offers during a lull in bus traffic. I climb into the backseat of his car—parked behind the tent—and he and Tina drive me the short distance to my cabin. They watch me unlock the padlock and go inside, and then they head back to the tent before the next bus arrives.

Toklat was crawling with bears last year. A ranger said this to me this morning, and now I repeat the words to myself as I picture the face of the earth like an animal hide, the vegetation like fur, the bears like fleas, rampaging in every direction. I keep thinking of the bear vanishing over the ridge, toward my cabin. I tell myself that nothing has changed. But something in my mind has shifted: Previously the bears were *out there,* a part of the landscape, not *here,* near my cabin. Still, I will have to go outside again eventually.

Finally, I head to the outhouse—carrying bear spray. But there is no bear to be seen, a rainbow stretches across the sky, and the fireweed continues to burn itself out in the brief Alaska summer.

"Did you see Fabio last night?" Ranger Bob asks me on the morning of day 6 when I arrive in the tent. He tells me that last night, when he and Tina took a drive to scope out a hiking location, they saw a bear they call Fabio—an old, thin, long-haired bear—on the road near my cabin. He's been around, Bob tells me, for all four of the summers that he and Tina have been coming to Toklat. I haven't seen Fabio, but I add him to my mental bear census.

I join Ranger Tina's discovery hike, and the dozen of us head into a gray, misty rain. Because the ground is wet, we eat lunch standing in the rain on a hillside. Ranger Tina tells us that usually at this point she hands out postcards and asks people to write something to themselves. She will mail the postcards, and in several weeks we will receive a message from ourselves, a different version of ourselves, the version that is out here in the wilderness today, and if we run across the card later, five or ten years from now, we will remember this day: stepping out of our lives to come to this place. But since it's raining, she waits to give us the postcards on the bus. I hold mine the whole ride back to Toklat. It's still blank when I get back to my cabin. I don't know the words I would speak to my future self from my current temporal and geographic position. I could write that I yearn for bears, but is that true? Perhaps I do not yearn for bears, but for what they represent. I want to step outside my cabin, that pocket of safety; I want to disembark from the park buses, those armored pods of civilization. I want to strip down to just myself and walk on my own two legs. Pared to my essence, I want to face the bear—or what the bear means. I yearn for something impossible: to peel away civilization from my being, to slip out of it like a discarded sock, to stare wilderness in the eyes.

On another discovery hike led by Ranger Greg, we pause to look over what he calls a bear dig: an area of ground squirrel burrows that have been ravaged, the ground gashed, clods flung in every direction. Grizzlies, he tells us, are the great diggers of the bear world. Later, when I stop by road camp to check my email, I find myself reading about bear diets. Adolph Murie, who called the ground squirrel "the staff of life" for the many Denali species that it feeds, wrote that it is a mere "side dish" for the grizzly. Then I'm lost again in research, learning about Russian scientists who removed the brains from Siberian ground squirrels at three different stages of hibernation to examine the neurons in the hippocampus. Squirrels in group A were in mid-hibernation. Squirrels in group B were in the shivered-back-to-normal-temperature sleeping state. And squirrels in group C were wide awake, one day post-hibernation. Compared to the fully awake squirrels in group C, the group A squirrels had shrunken neurons with fewer dendrites—the branchlike structures that receive messages from other neurons. The sleeping squirrels in group B, however, had rapidly replenished the missing dendrites. In fact, they had more connections in their brains than the active, awake squirrels of group C. In the awake squirrels' brains, many of these connections had been severed, pruned back. This dieback and overgrowth process happens repeatedly in the cold/hibernating warm/sleeping cycle.

Then I read about researchers in Germany who cut into the brains of hibernating European ground squirrels to learn more about Alzheimer's disease. The focus of their research was related to a protein with the unassuming name of tau. In the brains of people with Alzheimer's, the tau proteins become overburdened by phosphate molecules, which deform them and cause them to accumulate. It turns out this same process occurs in the hibernating brains of the squirrels, yet in the hours after waking, somehow the squirrels wipe their brains clean of the misshapen tau proteins.

I keep thinking about the ground squirrel that watched me on Thorofare Ridge, marveling that it could be somehow connected, even in a tenuous way, to Alzheimer's research. I can't make these disparate stories mesh in my mind, and yet scientists, creating their own narratives, weave together these storylines in astonishing ways. Before coming to Denali, I had read an article by biologist Paul Grobstein, and his words come back to me now:

> Scientific statements are . . . provisional stories, reflecting human perspectives, that get progressively less wrong. . . . Science is therefore fundamentally not about security but about doubt, not about knowing but about asking, not about certainty but about skepticism. Scientific stories are written not to be *believed* but to be understood, made use of as appropriate, and revised.

In his own schematic of the scientific method, a revision of the model so many of us are taught in elementary school, Grobstein introduces an element he calls "the crack," the spot where a scientist makes a choice, consciously or not, "to further pursue one or another way of several alternative ways of *making sense of the world*." It is here, Grobstein argues, that science is affected by "the individual temperament and cultural background" as well as the "creativity" of scientists. Some see this as a weakness, but Grobstein believes it is a major strength of science.

I think about Grobstein's idea of the "crack"—our subjectivity that begins with cultural background, personal temperament, and individual creativity, but that encompasses all of our life experiences. I imagine standing in the bottom of a rock crevice and peering up at the sky through the narrow fissure above me. The slice I can see is limited by the steep walls on either side, by where I find myself (in time and place), but it's also limited by my physical abilities of apprehension—my very senses that deliver all of the information I will ever have about the world. My observations of bears, my limited understanding of the mysterious subterranean lives of ground squirrels are but brief glimpses of totality. Each of us, peering through our own crack, tells a small part of the story. "The story of science is not, and cannot be, by itself the *view from everywhere*," writes Grobstein. "A different person, in a different time and place, might well tell a different story." Thinking about this, I understand something about the small bits of scientific research I am able to retrieve over the road camp's slow internet connection: It takes a brilliant imagination indeed to connect these creatures of the tundra who lay torpid underground for three-quarters of the year with the elderly human being who is losing his words, his memories, himself. Science can be masterful storytelling indeed.

In *Braiding Sweetgrass* Robin Wall Kimmerer writes of her first encounter in the 1970s with her college adviser, who wanted to know why she was majoring in botany. "I told him that I chose botany because I wanted to learn about why asters and goldenrod looked so beautiful together." The adviser shot down her aspirations, saying, "I must tell you *that* is not science." Kimmerer had wanted to become a botanist or a poet: "Since everyone told me I couldn't do both, I'd chosen plants." Many years later, Kimmerer understood that her adviser was offering her a narrow view of what science was and what it could do. "I circled right back to where I had begun, to the question of beauty. Back to the questions that science does not ask, not because they aren't important, but because science as a way of knowing is too narrow for the task," she writes. Her adviser was operating under the understanding that "since science separates the observer and the observed, by definition beauty could not be a valid scientific question."

Blending her training as a botanist, Indigenous ways of knowing the natural world, the color theory of art, and her poetic inclinations, Kimmerer eventually arrives at a new type of understanding. The question of why asters and goldenrod are beautiful together can be answered in myriad ways. In fact, researchers have found that the two flowers growing together attract more pollinators than when they grow apart. The bees, too, find the combination alluring. Kimmerer writes, "It's a testable hypothesis; it's a question of science, a question of art, and a question of beauty." She refuses to privilege one kind of knowledge over another. "When botanists go walking the forests and fields looking for plants, we say we are going on a *foray*," she writes. "When writers do the same, we should call it a *metaphoray*, and the land is rich in both. We need them both." These different ways of understanding the world, I realize, are different forms of storytelling. In my daily hikes I go on forays, and in my nightly thinking sessions—reading and writing for hours—I go on metaphorays. Both feel essential.

"Quick, go find the stamper!" a woman shouts to her son as they burst into the Eielson Visitor Center. They're being carried on the wave of passengers who have just gotten off a bus—and time is short. The boy, about twelve, heads directly for the passport cancelation station, where he stamps the official Eielson stamp onto the appropriate page in his National Parks Passport. I watch rangers at the information desk dispense maps, directions to the restroom, information about the bus schedules.

A chilly fog hangs in the air. Visitors stand at the enormous window that's meant to frame the mountain, only there's nothing there to see. An etching in the glass shows where Denali would be, if she were visible. Some take photos of the white bank of fog. Others photograph the large picture of the mountain that hangs on the wall: an image of what they almost saw, of what they could have seen, had they come on another day. It's day 7, and I haven't seen the mountain for three days now.

For many day-trippers, Eielson is the end of the line: The round-trip bus ride to mile 66 and back is a full eight hours. This is as far as they will go into the park and as close as they will get to the mountain. I watch the people milling about the window that frames the empty space, and I think about something Ranger Dan told me: that the mountain is even more present when she's not out. Obscured, ineffable, she becomes in their minds a specter, a possibility, looming larger in imagination than she ever does in reality. Because the idea of the mountain is more potent than an actual mountain. And maybe it's also true that I'm after not actual bears but the idea of bears. And the idea of bears for me has come to permeate every inch of landscape, every vista. Most of the bears I've seen—I'm up to fifteen now—are distant and two-dimensional, barely more than flat representations on a screen. But the bears in my imagination take away my breath. They come to me in my dreams. Almost everything about the bear is mightier than me: its bulk, its muscles, its fur, the weight of its bones, its teeth, its charisma, its solidness and comfort in the world, its claws—especially its claws, glinting in my dreams like sickles.

According to Alaska writer Sherry Simpson, people who encounter bears "soon realize that the bears living in their heads are not the same creatures walking the world around them." Is this why I seem to be having trouble seeing—really *seeing*—a bear? Because my mind is clouded over with a thousand ideas and myths and images of bears? Because I cannot make my forays and my metaphorays coalesce into a single image? Some bears "are trophies, some are meat. Some are predators, some are prey. Some are noble, some are nuisances, some are clowns," Simpson writes. "Most difficult to understand are those that are just bears, animals whose purposes and desires and lives belong only to themselves. Those are the bears most of us never see." And that, precisely, is the bear I want to see: the one that no one else sees.

On day 9—my last full day—I'm on a discovery hike in the East Fork River being led by Ranger Emily, and we are talking about bears. Emily is telling me why she thinks people are so fascinated by bears: Because they can eat us, and so in their presence, we no longer feel like we are at the top of the food chain. Because they're mysterious and there's so much we don't know about them. Because of the myriad and often contrary ways in which they are depicted—as cuddly stuffed animal versus murderous beast. Because they are our kin—they resemble us, or perhaps we resemble them, in body form, in diet—and because we have lived together—or near one another—for thousands of years. Where bears go, people go. In some Native American legends, humans are descended from bears, or bears morph into humans.

As we talk, I realize that my imagination has teemed with bears my entire life, from the earliest fairy tales I heard in Russian and then in English. The brown bear has been associated with Russia for centuries, and California—the place I spent my childhood and early adulthood—features a grizzly on its state flag and in its mythology, even though grizzlies have been gone from the state since the mid-1920s. In both of my languages, bears can be friendly and benevolent, with diminutives like Teddy and Misha, or they can be ferocious and menacing. When I got my driver's license, the first place I went, braving the freeway alone, was the natural history museum in the next city over, specifically to look at bears. I did not understand my compulsion to go stare at the frozen forms of taxidermied brown bears and polar bears, but it felt like a plunge into the wilds of adulthood. It felt necessary.

I have been lost in my own thoughts, and now we've hiked some distance, well out of sight of the park road. When we stop for a break, I pull out my water bottle and let my eyes wander over the hills of tundra to the west. Suddenly, my gaze snags on something: a bright blue tent, and on the next slope, a small orange one. Further in the distance I can just make out a third tent, tan with green accents. Just like that, the wilderness—or rather, my illusion of it—shimmers like a mirage, disintegrates. I am not in wilderness at all; I am surrounded by people. And the pristine vistas as seen from the park road—preserved by rules that require campers to be out of sight of the road—suddenly seem artificial, maintained so that tentative bus-riding tourists clutching big-lensed cameras can be secure in their illusion that they are seeing untrammeled nature, so that they don't get a tent in their photograph, so that the picture is not marred by the corrupting presence of humankind. But for me, suddenly, that illusion evaporates; Denali is crawling with people.

I think of Roderick Nash's concept of an environment's "carrying capacity": how well a place withstands human influence while still remaining wild. When too many people visit a wilderness, there comes a breaking point at which the place ceases to be wild, losing the very quality we were protecting. According to Nash, "This impact of wilderness lovers upon other wilderness lovers is the main reason why wilderness can be loved to death." Three tents do not make a mob. And yet, just as that first bear in Toklat made the whole region crawl with bears, so now does the presence of three tents transform this into too-crowded terrain, the wilderness version of a New York City street corner. The truth is, the landscape is crawling neither with bears nor with people—or at least no more than it ever has been since my arrival. It is my mind that crawls with bears and people, and that places them in opposition. The problem with wilderness—or my idea of it—is that I can have it only at the expense of others not having it. Wilderness is finite, a special condition of not seeing too many other people or the mark they make. Wilderness is the willful erasing—or at least the temporary concealing—of other members of my own species. With our superior brains, we have thought ourselves entirely out of the wild—the very world that birthed us and that is, or once was, our home. This is the paradox of wilderness: that we can destroy it by our very presence, and in the end, it is only an illusion anyway. But the bear knows no other state but wilderness; the bear is always in wilderness, or put another way, he has no grasp of wilderness as a concept because he does not make demarcations between the tame and the wild. He does not draw lines upon the globe separating himself from other living creatures, for the bear *is* wilderness. He carries it with him wherever he goes—and it is for this, perhaps, that I envy him most.

In my final bus ride back to Toklat, I see bears 17 and 18 in the distance. Then the driver, Elton, stops the bus when he spies another brown bear by the river tearing the ground apart with its massive claws. I see the rippling bulge of the shovel-shaped muscle in its back. The passengers all crowd to the bear side of the bus with cameras firing rapidly.

"He's probably after a ground squirrel," Elton says. Sometimes bears will pound the ground to flush the squirrels out, he adds. A typical bear in Denali will eat 100 to 150 ground squirrels per summer.

"They're like a Snickers bar for the bears," he says. "A nice little snack."

Suddenly, I understand something of the bear's impulse to rip apart the ground and pull the squirrel from its labyrinth—only I don't want to eat it, I want to *know* it. Human hunger to understand is nearly as strong as the other hungers of the body. I realize that while bears have lived in my mind always, arctic ground squirrels are newcomers; I had never thought of them at all, hadn't even known of them—except perhaps dimly—and their frantic, scurrying, hidden selves remain enigmas to me. My stories of bears are largely my own, rooted in a lifetime of imagining them, but my stories of ground squirrels are recently appropriated from others. That was why I had turned to science to learn their stories. What's more, arctic ground squirrels do not make for riveting campfire tales; no one ever asks me for my rodent stories. An encounter with a squirrel hardly makes for a satisfying "man versus nature" plot. Facing an arctic ground squirrel does not feel like a quintessential wilderness experience, even though the squirrel is just as wild as the bear.

It's my last evening in the cabin, and I'm rereading an essay by William Cronon. He writes:

> If nature dies because we enter it, then the only way to save nature is to kill ourselves. The absurdity of this proposition flows from the underlying dualism it expresses. . . . The tautology gives us no way out: if wild nature is the only thing worth saving, and if our mere presence destroys it, then the sole solution to our own unnaturalness, the only way to protect sacred wilderness from profane humanity, would seem to be suicide.

Is the extreme form of seeking wilderness a wishing away of my own existence? Have I come here, in part, to get away not just from other people, but from myself?

This thinking is not conducive to what lies ahead: my leaving the wilderness, returning to my regularly scheduled life. I keep reading. "Without our quite realizing it, wilderness tends to privilege some parts of nature at the expense of others," Cronon writes. "If it isn't hundreds of square miles big, if it doesn't give us God's eye views or grand vistas, if it doesn't permit us the illusion that we are alone on the planet, then it really isn't natural. It's too small, too plain, or too crowded to be authentically wild." Soon I will be returning to my modest New England landscapes, to the classroom and student essays, to the cooking of meals in a well-appointed kitchen and the shuttling of children to swim team and piano lessons, to gridlocked traffic and the wails of sirens on city streets, to the diminutive wild of my tiny backyard with its robins and blue jays, chipmunks and tree squirrels.

These are my thoughts as I venture outside into the night, headed for the outhouse.

In the morning, after a restless last night at the cabin, I make one last trek to the Toklat tent, where I find Ranger Bob on duty. We say our goodbyes, and I leave with him the postcard that Tina gave me on our hike. Instead of addressing it to myself, I've addressed it to her. *Thank you*, I've written. *I will never forget that day.* I've filled the card with words, but I make no record for myself of what they say.

Now, with all of my gear and excess food packed in Ranger Dan's car, we're headed east, to park headquarters, where I'll spend my final night in Denali. As I watch the landscape spool by one final time, we talk about bears. Dan tells me that he used to lead a ranger program on bears, and that he would begin by describing his own bear encounter, drawing the story out and making it as dramatic as possible. The entire encounter lasted maybe thirty seconds, but it took him ten minutes to tell the story. It's not even a remarkable bear story—he encountered some bears and then they left him alone, which is actually how the majority of bear stories go—but the point is to have a bear story. The point of seeing a bear is having a story to tell afterward.

As he is talking, I think about telling him my own bear story, so fresh in my mind. I think about shaping an animal into words. My story goes like this:

My twentieth bear came to me my final night in the cabin, when I was walking to the outhouse. I was thinking about leaving Alaska, about returning to Connecticut, when I stepped blithely around the corner of my cabin—and there, thirty feet away, coming out of the vegetation, was the bear, its coat glowing burnt sienna in the twilight. When I appeared and then stopped dead in my tracks, the bear rose up onto its hind legs to see me better, the dark pits of its eyes fixating on me, pinning me to the landscape, to the fireweed and night sky, to the wilderness. I was close enough that I could see the subtle variations in color of its coat, from strawberry blond to mahogany, and the gentle rise and fall of its massive chest as it breathed. I was close enough to see it apprehending me, its mind working on me like a problem that needed solving. For some time—ten seconds? a minute?—we stared into each other's eyes. *This is what it is to be seen by a bear*, I thought—and it was nothing like merely seeing a bear. Suddenly, I was stripped down, a weak, two-legged creature completely at the bear's mercy. But that was not the right word. Bears don't have mercy. But looking into those eyes, I understood that bears have will, that they are self-willed like the land. I was at the bear's will. To be seen by a bear was to be rendered to flesh, to muscle and bone; it was to be overpowered in every way, by body and bulk, an intellect that is keener and more alien than I ever imagined. To be seen by a bear was to be put in place on the chain of being, which at its essence is the food chain. And I was clearly below the bear, for I had nothing: no bear spray, no weapon, and even my sneakers were untied. *This,* I thought, *is to enter the wilderness. At last.*

I did none of the things I was supposed to: I didn't raise my arms to look bigger, I didn't talk to the bear, I didn't shout, "Hey, Mr. Bear, fine night for a stroll! How about we both go on our merry ways?" Simply, I looked at the bear, and the bear looked at me. And then slowly, I backed away from the bear, reversing my steps to the cabin. The bear only watched me. When my feet hit the porch, I lunged for the door and crashed inside. Then I stood there, my back against the shut door, my jellied legs trembling, waiting for the bear's bulk to come slamming against the wall. I watched the windows, waiting for its massive skull to appear there and its dark eyes to seek me out and for its mighty paw to smash through glass. I waited for a monster bear, a mythical beast whose aim was to devour me. I waited for a bear that never came, a bear that didn't exist at all. All night, even after I was in bed, I waited, and nothing happened. The bear that saw me did only that: see me. Then it continued on its business of being a bear. The whole episode was but a chance encounter between two species—like a billion others, utterly unremarkable. We simply left one another in peace.

I tell none of this to Ranger Dan.

"This may be our oldest, truest survival skill: the ability to tell stories and to learn from each other's stories," writes Simpson. "In some ways, Alaska is nothing but stories." And an archetypal Alaska story needs a bear in it. Yet a life is not the same as a story—not even close—but a story is all I can make of another being's life, and when we are speaking of other species, that story is not just imprecise but sometimes fatally wrong. Bears have no need for my stories, and to turn their lives into one is to misapprehend them entirely, and it is also to surrender to the impulse that makes us most human. In an encounter with any wild animal, a rift exists between the event itself and the story we tell of it afterward. The bear sees me as a creature, something to be apprehended and appraised entirely within the context of preserving and furthering that one immeasurably valuable thing he has in his possession, his life, and I see him as a danger, as something that threatens my own life—in that way, we are both creatures simply trying to live—but later, in the long, distorting hindsight with which we hold onto and apprehend most of the events of our lives, the bear will become story, defanged and declawed and disempowered and worn to harmlessness with my words, something utterly foreign to what he actually is: the bulk of flesh and bone and blood and hide, the intellect that nestles deep in his alien bear brain. Words are never as sharp as teeth or claws, for by my very ability to tell a story, I have given away its ending: that I came to no lasting harm, that I am still here.

For two years after my time in Denali, I speak little of the bears I saw, believing somehow that if I don't speak of them, I will be able to maintain their true essence, their astounding bearness, in my mind. But as soon as I name the bear, I will occlude my vision of him; he will become *my bear* and not his own bear. He will become the kind of bear that we see, not the kind of bear that we don't see.

But it is words—written and spoken—that make the best, most lasting containers for our memories, so in the end, before my memory of the bears grows fuzzy and distorted, I capitulate to that most basic human urge: I tell my bear story. My twentieth bear finally becomes that which I have resisted by remaining silent, that which I have been protecting him from with my self-willed muteness; he becomes the only thing I am equipped with my human brain to make of him: a story. And no matter how many times I tell it, how many details I include or leave out, how long I stretch it to spark wonder and dread in my listener's heart, how viciously I tear at the veil of wilderness that obstructs my vision, it will not be the bear's story—it can never be the bear's story—but remains ever only my own.

We gaze out at the world from behind a scrim of culture, of language, hampered by the limitations of our weak senses, sometimes barely making out the shapes on the other side. When I look out at the country of bears and declare it untrammeled wilderness, when I see the world split into the civilized and the wild, I am perpetuating stories that I have inherited from centuries of human thought stretching back through the Western tradition from biblical notions of wilderness to the Puritans and on to the present day—a lineage that encourages the simple dichotomies of tame and wild, self and other, and that neglects other stories, especially ones that blur or complicate or negate these distinctions. And when I look at arctic ground squirrels and demand of them stories that can solve the problem of the aging human brain, I am equally under the sway of a powerful narrative, one that holds great authority in our contemporary world: that of science as absolute wisdom, a rational and objective way to know the world, conclusive and without reproach. It is a way of knowing that often arrogantly declares other stories—especially ones grounded in religion or Indigenous knowledge—as archaic, superstitious, unenlightened. In any story I tell, I am getting at but a minuscule portion of a greater whole.

If Alaska is nothing but stories, as Simpson claims, these stories reveal as much about ourselves as they do about the character of Alaska. "Story—sacred and profane—is perhaps *the* main cohering force in human life," writes Jonathan Gottschall in *The Storytelling Animal: How Stories Make Us Human*. "Story is the center without which the rest cannot hold." Our theory of mind means we instinctively understand that our experiences differ from those of others. As soon as we look upon another creature with the question, *What is it like to be you?*, we start composing stories. And our impulse to study other life forms, to try to burrow our way into the brain of a bear or a hibernating squirrel, is in essence our desire to claim their stories, or parts of them, and make them our own. The story of human beings is the story of a species that tells stories. Storytelling, our "oldest, truest survival skill," is simply how we know the world. We cannot have forays without metaphorays. I will keep telling stories and cultivating my storytelling faculties, recognizing that my vision is but a version, a narrow slice glimpsed through a crack, a distorted image apprehended through the meager faculties of my human mind.

Antelope Island State Park

PANORAMA OF A LIFE

July 1996

That day, I was in the supermarket for cat food and cigarettes—the bare necessities of my desperation—when a glossy image on a backpacking magazine stopped me: a gnarled tree on a barren slope, an austere peak rising beyond. *There. That's where I want to go.* I splurged and bought the four-dollar magazine, along with two cans of cat food, a pack of Marlboro Reds.

At my parents' house I showed the magazine to my brother Alex. *There. That's where I want to go.* He would handle logistics. At sixteen, he didn't yet drive, but he was my navigator, my companion. We had recently gone to Yosemite and Kings Canyon. He was good at reading maps, at planning. At twenty-one, I was good at living on a precipice, acting on impulse.

I lived five miles away in the ruin of a past life: a one-bedroom apartment with a beanbag, a bookcase, a narrow cot, a cat named Chaos, and six cans of food (beef broth, pear halves, diced tomatoes, green beans, two cream-of-mushroom soups). In the broom closet albino tentacles unfurled from an abandoned sack of potatoes.

I worked the 6 p.m. to midnight agate shift on the sports desk. *Agate*: the small typeface of the statistics that densely fill the Scoreboard page. I compiled the stats from wire services, took box scores from high school and college games over the phone, chased late scores on deadline. I was the only female on the sports desk. A lot of the guys were just out of college, a couple of years older than me, full-timers. I was a part-timer, working thirty hours a week. They were in it for the long haul, but I was already on my way out the door, as soon as I figured out where I was going.

Some nights I went out drinking with the guys after deadline, and other nights I sat in my bean bag with Chaos, scribbling something I called *my novel.* I wanted to rush into life headlong, impetuously. I wanted to act without thinking, to plan nothing. Because planning had failed me. I had planned an entire life, with a boyfriend of five years. I still had the engagement ring and wedding bands, I had our apartment and the potatoes we bought, I had the cat we adopted; but the boyfriend was gone, along with his furniture.

There. That's where I want to go. Alex figured out the rest. Our destination: Great Basin National Park, 530 miles from Riverside, California, an eight-hour drive.

August 2016

That day—with my husband at work, the kids at day camp—I was writing in the library. On my way out, a glossy cover in the used book sale arrested me. I immediately recognized the silhouette of the peak, the twisting trees: Great Basin National Park. It was the shiny, photo-filled type of book sold in visitor center gift shops. I asked its price. Two dollars, the librarian told me. I bought it on the spot.

It seemed like serendipity, for I was already planning to go back to Great Basin, with Alex and my kids. I now lived in Connecticut, Alex in Nebraska, where he worked in logistics. He planned the itinerary. I told my kids, eight and eleven, about visiting the park in the nineties. I told them about climbing Wheeler Peak, bristlecone pines. Back then, I said, their uncle and I just did things, without planning. And things just worked out. They always worked out: The proof was in my continued existence.

Whenever anyone asked me what my favorite national park was of the couple dozen I've visited, I always answered: Great Basin. "What's there?" someone once asked. "Bristlecone pines," I said. "Wheeler Peak." *My heart,* I thought.

And now, twenty years later, I was taking my kids there.

July 1996

We were driving right into that place on the magazine cover in my Honda Civic hatchback, Leonard Cohen booming from the speakers. These details mattered. The car was barely a year old, which meant my car payment was a third of my monthly earnings, but it also meant I had a reliable car I could go anywhere in, with a CD player. Since the boyfriend left, I listened to Leonard Cohen obsessively, until I knew by heart his dark, fraught lyrics, which were a mirror of my own mind. Leonard Cohen knew things about me I didn't know myself.

We stopped at a Vegas buffet. Alex told me we might be able to see Vegas from the top of Wheeler Peak, if conditions were right. But from Vegas, we could see only garish lights, swarms of people.

We kept going. I thought about the boyfriend. For most of our time together, we had lived at home, on the same street three houses apart. I was fifteen, he sixteen, when we met. He was exactly ten months older, a grade ahead. One day we would marry; the engagement ring on my finger proved it.

Then came apartment life: cigarette butts pouring out of ashtrays, Mickey's Big Mouth bottles strewn across carpet, network TV blaring, unwashed dishes in the sink, a black scum coating the tub. We argued and fell silent and made up and staggered to bed to do it all again. We had all but dropped out of school: He was still nominally enrolled at the community college, and I was flunking out of the state university to which I had transferred. The school was too far away, my nights too full of deadlines and booze, and I didn't see any point in taking libel law or macroeconomics. If I finished my degree, I could have a full-time newspaper job, but every time I tried this future on for size, it didn't fit. And if I married the boyfriend, I would become the person I had planned to be—but I could neither become this person nor imagine an alternative self. I could only loathe the way things were: how the boyfriend complained about his department store job but did nothing about it, how his junky Karmann Ghias and Bugs were constantly breaking down, how he let his hair and goatee grow long, how he cussed and kept his clothes in moldering piles, how he drank and drank and smoked and smoked, how we brought out the worst in each other.

Still, I kept agreeing to go places with him: Volkswagen car shows, noisy dance clubs, Disneyland, rock concerts. We saw big-name bands that left so little impression on me that I can't possibly name them. All I remember is the terrible press of people, the screaming, the sloshing beer, the distant stage where figures thrashed and noise blared. All I remember is wanting it to be over.

But now, this smooth unspooling of desolate highway, the low croon of Leonard Cohen's voice, the steering wheel in my command: This was what I wanted. Finally, I was becoming myself. Or I was about to: I was on the cusp of something.

When we stopped in a tiny town for gas, another traveler—a lone man about my age—was finishing up on the other side of our single shared pump. "Leonard Cohen," he said with a nod. "Cool." And then he was gone before I could respond. That I would find a kindred spirit—someone who could identify Leonard Cohen from the wisp of a lyric blowing out of an open car door, *There's a shoulder where death comes to cry*—in the middle of the desert, felt like serendipity, a confirmation that I belonged right here, in Caliente, Nevada, right now, on this bright summer midday at the tail-end of a century, a millennium.

Take this waltz, Leonard Cohen insisted. *It's yours now, it's all that there is.* In the passenger seat, Alex was unfolding a map.

"Do you want to drive on the Loneliest Road in America?" he asked.

"Yes," I said. "Definitely. There's nothing I want more."

But the boyfriend kept tugging at me. I had thought it would never end, but it ended so easily, not in cataclysm but in anticlimax. It ended simply like this: one night in mid-January, after I turned twenty-one but before he turned twenty-two, as we sat on the sofa downing beers and chain-smoking and staring at vapidity on the TV, I turned to him and calmly said: *I can't do this anymore. It's over.* I told him: *Leave.*

The next day he—along with all his furniture—vanished while I was at work. It felt like such a clean, painless break: like a cleaving with a knife so sharp that it hardly draws blood.

August 2016

After spending a night at a ski resort at 7,500 feet in order to acclimate, we were finally there, the four of us packed into Alex's Honda Civic, driving around the loop at Wheeler Peak Campground, at 10,000 feet.

"That's where we stayed before," Alex said, pointing at an empty spot with a concrete parking pad. "Remember?"

I nodded, but I didn't remember. I looked at the trees, the mountain terrain. It seemed familiar only in that it looked like a lot of the places I had visited in the past twenty years. Bristlecone pines and Wheeler Peak: that was all I remembered. A magazine cover and Leonard Cohen, a gone boyfriend: what I remembered.

We chose a spot, and Alex paid for three nights. Then: unloading, setting up camp, making a fire, preparing food, planning the next day's activities, slithering into sleeping bags. It all seemed tedious, unremarkable. Had we done all of this before? I remembered none of it.

My son was restless all through the night, throwing his body across mine. Abruptly, he sat up and said, "I want to go out and look at the stars."

I watched from the tent as he wandered around outside, looking up. The sky was smeared in a messy abundance of stars.

"There aren't this many stars in Connecticut," he told me.

"There are more stars here than anywhere else. That's one of the reasons we came here." I told him fibs, and then we went back to sleep.

July 1996

From our campground we stumbled on a trail that led us to bristlecone pines—the twisted trees of the magazine cover. Later, we found ourselves at a ranger program. The ranger, a couple of years older than me, enthusiastically talked about the trees: where they grew, how incredibly old they were. Watching him, suddenly I thought: *That could be me.* I could be the one telling astonishing stories about trees.

After the talk, I approached the ranger. "How do you become a park ranger?"

He smiled, a little patronizingly, and told me about how he had gone to college and majored in political science, adding that rangers come from many different backgrounds.

Back in the tent, I kept thinking about the ranger, the bristlecone pines. If some of those trees had stood for millennia, what did a grandfather dying matter? What did a boyfriend with cancer matter? Because those things had happened too.

In late January, a couple of weeks after the boyfriend left, my grandfather was hospitalized with colon cancer. In April, he was dead.

And two years prior, when I had just turned nineteen, but the boyfriend had not yet turned twenty, and we were still both living at home, attending community college, he was diagnosed with testicular cancer. Suddenly, I was thrust into a Technicolor drama, my life a cancer montage. Scene: driving my boyfriend to the sperm bank every two days, where in a closet-sized room stocked with porn magazines he masturbated into a plastic cup, so that he could be a father one day. Scene: the moments that took on an elongated quality—time turned to taffy—as I sat in the hospital waiting room beside his mother during his orchiectomy. Scene: my vigil at his bedside, every day, as the weeks of radiation left him enervated, barely able to say more than two or three words. Scene: when he seemed to sleep, I worked on our classwork, writing his papers and my own. I would keep both of us afloat. If we could beat this, we could beat anything. If we stared death in the face and triumphed, if I maintained our grades, we would be together forever.

Afterward, we felt relief when he was declared cancer-free at six months, then at another six months, and another, but relief is a fleeting, weak emotion. The new mundanity of our lives crushed us. We began to drink and smoke more. If you could get cancer and lose a testicle at nineteen, there were no guarantees you'd make it another year, let alone into the next century. We lived a life out of which the color was leaching. Those cancer months had been lived in ultra-high contrast, the color saturation turned all the way up, every moment lurid and fraught. And everything that followed was watery and pale, blanched of meaning.

August 2016

In late afternoon, as we started out for the bristlecone pines, my son fell behind. Uncharacteristically lethargic, he walked ever more slowly, stopping every seventy steps, ignoring my urgings to make it a hundred steps between rests.

"It's so steep," he gasped. But it wasn't.

"Come on," his sister said, grabbing his elbow. "You can do

this." She began to make up alliterative sayings to buoy his spirits. "Sadly, the stupid spelunker was stabbed by surreptitiously sharp stalagmites."

My son suddenly stopped, dropped to his knees, and vomited.

"Uh oh!" my daughter yelled. "Altitude sickness!"

How had I not seen it before? The sleepless night, lack of appetite, lethargy: All of this pointed to the cause of his malaise. This had happened before. On a trip to the Snowy Range in Wyoming, where we had camped at 10,000 feet, my son's altitude sickness had forced us to evacuate to 7,000 feet. This time, we thought we had done it right, spending a night at the ski resort to acclimate, but clearly, we hadn't.

Aborting the hike, we commenced the mincing walk back to camp, where Alex started a fire, preparing to cook sausages and hamburgers, while I lay beside my son in the tent. Maybe a rest would be enough. I kept telling myself this.

Suddenly, he sat up alertly, just as he had the night before when he went out to look at stars. "I need to throw up," he said, lurching for the zippered door. I opened it in time for him to stick his head out and vomit on the rainfly.

Outside, dark clouds gathered as Alex and my daughter busied themselves with the fire.

"He's not better!" I called to them. I helped my son stagger to a stump where he collapsed and kept retching.

Alex looked over at us, then up at the clouds. At that moment, a chute opened in the sky, dumping hailstones onto our heads.

July 1996

We went about climbing Wheeler Peak all wrong: sleeping in, having a leisurely breakfast, starting out late. I wore shorts and a fanciful Cat in the Hat sweatshirt. Alex carried a gallon jug of water in a pillowcase slung over his shoulder. We took almost no food and a couple ninety-nine-cent Walmart rain ponchos for protection against the elements. We walked slowly up the trail without any concern for time.

According to the National Park Service website, the hike is 8.6

miles round trip with a nearly 3,000-foot elevation gain, climbing to 13,000 feet. "This hike should be started very early in the day because of the risk of afternoon storms," the site warns. At the time, we either didn't know this or we didn't care. Even if we knew the numbers, we didn't know what they meant in practical terms. Fewer than twenty-four hours before, we had traveled from 800 feet to 10,000 without a thought about acclimatization.

As I trudged along, I thought about how I might be able to glimpse Vegas from the top, which led irrevocably back to the boyfriend. A year ago—after the cancer but before the apartment—we took a trip to Vegas. He was twenty-one, I twenty. Everything about the trip felt forced. We ate at buffets, walked the Strip, drank, gambled. I worried about being carded, but I never was. I wore a form-fitting silver sweater and tight jeans. My long blonde hair swished against my back as I walked. I looked the way I thought I was supposed to look. I did the things I was supposed to do. Wasn't this what adults did? Wasn't this having fun?

Alex and I talked occasionally, but mostly we hiked in silence. Sometimes, I became so lost in the labyrinth of my thoughts that I barely saw the world around me: trees, rocks, trail. Nothing about this hike felt dangerous. I had already stared danger in the face: a boyfriend with cancer who didn't die, a grandfather with cancer who did. In the end, I lost them both anyway. Nothing seemed dangerous now. We were climbing a mountain in ignorance and stupidity, and so far, it was working out.

At some point, when I wasn't paying attention, the sky above us turned into a menacing bruise, and thunder rolled in the distance.

August 2016

We evacuated in the hailstorm. My son vomited into a bag in the backseat while the three of us broke down the tent and threw things into the car willy-nilly. The campfire roared on despite the hail, so we had to douse it with our potable water. When we couldn't fit everything into the car, we decided to leave with what we had and find another campground before sunset. The first campground we tried was closed, the second full. Finally, we found a spot at the Baker Creek

Campground, at 7,500 feet. As the sun was slipping toward the horizon, we hastily unfurled the tent and got my son inside.

After emptying the car, Alex made another trip back to our old camp to collect all we'd left behind. My daughter began to explore, and I peeked in at my son, who slept peacefully.

As I snapped pictures of the claret sunset, my daughter climbed onto a fallen log, which immediately started to roll out from under her, and for a moment she executed what looked like a carefully choreographed jig, until she lost her balance, flew off, and landed in a pile of rocks.

"I didn't hit my head!" she cried. "I didn't break my teeth!" Just four months before, she had sailed over the handlebars of her bicycle and landed face-first on concrete, smashing off both of her front teeth.

"OK, good," I breathed, moving toward her.

"Ow, ow ow!" she suddenly cried. "My arm!"

July 1996

When the thunderstorms started, we put on the flimsy rain ponchos, and we kept going. Great cracks of light opened in the sky, accompanied by reverberating booms. We were not above tree line yet, but the trees were getting sparse and stunted. The menacing gray wedge of mountain lay ahead—all rock, no vegetation, with patches of snow and ice. As the lightning speared the ridge, we walked on. I don't remember feeling worry or alarm. I remember just putting one foot in front of another.

The thunderstorm ended, but we still had the formidable ridge to ascend. I thought about the boyfriend, how the hardest part was not the initial breaking up but the keeping apart. We were too much of a habit with one another. About once a month, we relapsed. One of us was bored: I paged him, or he called me. We ended up going out drinking, spending the night together. We always agreed it was a one-time thing, a part of the process. We agreed that someday, our binges would end.

A couple months after the breakup, when my grandfather was still dying, we were at a bar when I said, "Let's go to Food-4-Less and buy the two biggest steaks we can find and take them back to the apartment and cook them." So we did.

After eating, I looked the boyfriend in the eye and said, "Let's go to Vegas and get married."

He studied me. "The worst part is, I think you almost believe what you're saying."

"I do believe it!" I cried. And I did—or I tried to. Maybe marriage was what we had been missing. Maybe this ultimate yoking of our lives was what we needed. On a whim my grandmother had agreed to marry my grandfather in a Vegas wedding chapel—because he had been pestering her. She married him to make him shut up. And her marriage had lasted through six kids, over half a century—to this very moment, when she was on her way to widowhood, nursing my grandfather through his last days. And she had been even younger than I was when she married. By the time she was my age, she was a mother.

"Look," I said. "Someday, when you're eighty years old and you're looking back on this night, you're going to regret not going through with it. You know why? Because people regret what they didn't do more than what they did do."

The boyfriend studied me again. As I talked, I tried to convince myself that my impetuous Vegas wedding idea would save the relationship, but I knew that wasn't the truth. What I was imagining had nothing to do with the boyfriend. Instead, I pictured myself telling the story of my Vegas wedding to Alex, the guys at work. I wanted to mystify people. I wanted to mystify myself.

The boyfriend balked. No, he said. This was not a good idea.

"Ideas not acted upon are worse than no ideas at all," I told him.

"That doesn't even make sense," he said. "You can't compare something that exists with something that doesn't."

I was tired of the conversation. When I was with the boyfriend, I became a person who swung erratically between two extremes: All or nothing. Love or hate. Smothered or abandoned. If we were not to be married, I never wanted to see him again.

And besides, my goal was not to be married, but rather to *have been* married. The whole point of a Vegas wedding was semantic: the word *ex-boyfriend* was not potent enough to contain our story. When

I told people I had an ex-boyfriend, they heard a mild, adolescent word, describing an ephemeral crush. They did not see the violent rending of two lives. They did not see the five years that we cleaved to one another: the fights, the drinking, the violence of our passions, the cancer. I wanted to make him more firmly mine—I wanted to yoke myself to him forever, in law, in language, so that I would have an *ex-husband*. I wanted to be a divorced woman at twenty-one. I wanted language that expressed the ravishment of having and then losing him.

But he wasn't going for it. He had no need for an ex-wife. And I was sick of him.

"Leave," I told him. "Please. Just leave." And he did.

But that wasn't the end either. We saw each other more times after that—I don't remember how many. I don't know how many hours we spent sitting sadly together in bars with nothing to say to one another. I don't even remember the last time.

August 2016

For the second time that evening, we were breaking up camp and evacuating—this time in the dark. And this time, my son was helping pack the car while my daughter sat at the picnic table clutching her arm. Was it broken? We had no way of knowing. My son, fully recovered after an hour at lower elevation, had scampered around camp while Alex stood on the picnic table—the only place he could get a signal—and googled elbow injuries. Periodically, he showed me images of arm bones on his phone. We took off my daughter's sweater but concluded only that her elbow looked swollen. She refused to move it.

Google told us worst-case scenarios: nerve damage, injured growth plates. Alex started searching for urgent care facilities. The nearest was an emergency room in Delta, Utah, a hundred miles away. We called and spoke with a nurse who told us what we already knew: There was no way to diagnose an elbow injury over the phone.

We got to the hospital just before midnight. My daughter was the only patient. X-rays were taken and sent to a radiologist in Provo while a doctor moved my daughter's arm and declared she had good range of motion. Then the radiologist's report came back: It was a contusion, not a break. One nurse wrapped my daughter's arm in a compression bandage and offered ice and Tylenol while the other nurse called around to find us a hotel room.

That's how we found ourselves munching hard bagels after midnight at a Days Inn in Delta, Utah. *This was not the plan,* I told myself. We were now a hundred miles from where I wanted to be. Everything seemed needlessly complicated, fraught with danger.

July 1996

This is when I'm supposed to have some great revelation, I thought, shivering on the gusty peak, looking out for hundreds of miles. Alex pointed in the direction of Vegas, but we couldn't see it, not really. Maybe there was a smudge there in the mist and clouds. But I didn't need to see Vegas from the top of a mountain to picture myself there: the twenty-year-old in a metallic sweater who walked so listlessly alongside the boyfriend, then the twenty-one-year-old who might have ended up at a wedding chapel in order to gain an ex-husband and a history. I saw those other selves, and I wished them goodbye. *Goodbye to you,* I thought. *Goodbye to you.*

In another direction, the sky was dark, clouds like iron fingers reaching for the desert. It was raining there. And somewhere else, the land was bathed in golden-pink sunshine. I could see it all from the top. But no revelation came to me—only the weary feeling that I would have to live with myself for the rest of my life. I could tell boyfriends to leave, I could climb mountains, but I couldn't escape myself.

Alex called me over to something he found among the rocks: a battered metal mailbox that contained the summit's register. Here, climbers had written their names, their hometowns, their thoughts upon reaching the peak. I riffled through the curled pages. Bruce wrote that he was *so high.* On another page, the Johnson family announced their presence. Two boys signed their names, followed by their ages, eight and ten. At the very bottom, one more name appeared, in small, tidy handwriting: *Eileen, just the mommy.*

The words made me angry. *Just the mommy.* If she had hauled herself all the way up here, she was more than just a mommy. She should take credit, proclaim herself a person, sans self-deprecating postscript. She was not just a mother who followed her children up mountains. I was certain of it. The rarefied air, the austere environment devoid of clutter, barren even of trees, stripped you down until you were your most essential self. *You are not just the mommy,* I said back to her. *You are someone who climbs mountains.* And that's who I was, too—at least for today. I was a person who climbed mountains. It felt like a sturdier identity than I had inhabited in months, years—maybe ever.

"Are you going to sign it?" Alex asked.

I rooted the pencil stub out of the mailbox. Turning to the next blank page, I wrote something. I don't remember what—probably just the date, our names, our hometown. Maybe I wrote: *I am a person who climbs mountains.* But probably I didn't. And then we headed back down.

August 2016

Sitting in camp in the glare of full sun, I looked out at the desolate landscape of Antelope Island in the Great Salt Lake and watched my children flanking their uncle as they crunched across salty ground that festered with dirty clouds of gnats. They were going to investigate an enormous, rusted buoy that looked like it had washed ashore in another epoch. My daughter carried her injured elbow in a sling, an ice pack tucked inside. My disappointment at ending up here was palpable. I didn't even know of the existence of Antelope Island until Alex had found it on his phone the night before when we were still eating stale bagels in Delta.

"How does Antelope Island sound?" he had asked.

It didn't sound appealing to me, but the kids were intrigued. Yes, they wanted to go to an island in the middle of an ancient lake of salt. Who didn't? And there would be bison there! For them, this was a serendipitous turn of events. Alex laid out the logistics of the situation: We had only one more night of camping before we were supposed to head back to Salt Lake City anyway. Great Basin was simply too far in the wrong direction. There was no going back.

In high spirits, Alex was finally able to make a campfire and cook the meat we'd been hauling around in the cooler. And he had no special attachment to Great Basin. He was willing to go back because I wanted to—but he was just as content walking on a briny beach, looking at rusted relics.

July 1996

There was so much I didn't know. If I could encounter my old self, striding blithely across that landscape, I am not sure what I would say to her.

Maybe I would tell her that I would not become a park ranger. Instead, seven years later, in graduate school, I would write my first work of creative nonfiction, about bristlecone pines, and it would be published. And later still, I would read it aloud to my kids before taking them to Great Basin. I would tell her: *That is what happened to you in Great Basin. You started to become a writer. You started to become the person you will be.*

Maybe I would tell her that to go to a place is not to visit a location on a map but to visit yourself in that place and sometimes even to visit your past selves. To visit a place is to see who you are and what is important to you refracted back through the lens of landscape. Maybe I have never seen Great Basin at all but merely myself in it—and when I came back twenty years later, I was not really visiting the place as much as I was visiting my former self. But my children would never see her, the person I was seeking. They saw bits of the terrain, which impressed them little. They know Great Basin only as a place of sickness and injury, aborted expectations. They know it as a place I once visited and became inexplicably attached to, back in the dimness of the past century, in the impetuous nineties when I was nobody's mother.

Maybe I only wanted the panorama of my life to stretch across this one landscape, to imbue the trees and mountain with all that has been significant to me. I wanted to anchor two posts in the ground, two decades apart, and unfurl the years of my life between them, a banner of all that I had done, all I had become. I wanted a landscape onto which I could drape my life. *Look how far I have come.*

And I failed, but I would have failed even if I had dragged my children to the top of that mountain. Revelations cannot be orchestrated. Even if we had seen the trees, been on the peak, these experiences would have been pale facsimiles. They would have been only tired nostalgia, not the primacy of first encounter. Maybe I would have stood again on the peak, waiting for revelation, squinting to see Vegas. Maybe I would have written in the register, after my children's names: *not just the mommy*. Maybe I would have written: *I am still a person who climbs mountains.* Or: *We are diminished by our own success.* Because the promise of the self I might be, the nascent becoming of the twenty-one-year-old me, would always be greater than the person I actually became. Becoming always trumps being.

I might tell her, my vanished self, something of the future—that I would marry and learn moderation, that the measure of a relationship is not in the violence of its passion—but I would not tell her that the goodbye of the mountaintop was also a goodbye to the boyfriend, a forever goodbye. I would not tell her that I would only ever see him once more in this world—at his wedding in two years. That I would not invite him to my own wedding, two years after that. We would not exchange birth announcements when our children were born. We would be no one at all to one another, for years, until he died of cancer at thirty-five. Three thousand miles away, I would not even learn of his death for a year. *Good-bye to you.* Maybe, in part, I wanted to return, years later, to whisper those words to him from that peak. But I would not reveal this future to my past self. The blanching effects of time are also a mercy.

August 2016

On a whim, I decided to take my kids on a nighttime hike to look for scorpions. After listening to a ranger talk and being issued ultraviolet lights—just one per family because the program was popular and the lights in short supply—dozens of us spread out across the island's grasslands, shining lights under bushes, seeking out the blue-green glow of the scorpions' exoskeletons.

"It's like the nineties, Mom," my daughter suddenly said. "We didn't plan this. We're just doing things."

It was true. I had forgotten how to be impetuous, how to let things just happen. I dropped back, let my kids lead the way. They walked close together, holding hands, their efforts earnest, determined. *This is what they will remember*, I thought, stopping. *This.* I looked out over the shapes moving in all directions. In the twilight, people looked alike, with no distinguishing features, except size.

"If you find one, be sure to let others know!" the ranger's voice rang out.

When I realized I had allowed my kids to get away from me, a mild panic seized my heart. They weren't lost, exactly, since they were among the people streaming around me, but I also didn't know exactly where they were. I began to walk in circles, peering into the faces of strangers. There were so many kids, none of them mine. I considered going to the ranger, saying: *I lost my kids.* But they were here, somewhere. I just had to look harder.

Suddenly, I thought: Would I one day, years from now, feel an urge to return to this place I had never wanted to go? Would I come to search for my lost self, my lost children, my lost self looking for my lost children? Were they really the ones lost? After all, they had each other and our light—I was the one alone, in darkness. Were these sloping grasslands on the rim of an ancient briny lake the new topography onto which I was writing my current self, my hopes for the future? Was this new landscape that I had resisted the panorama for a new life—unknown, untested, but just as astonishing? Was this the place of a new becoming?

"We found one over here!" the ranger called, her voice a magnet, pulling the wandering people in her direction.

I turned in circles, looking at the dark shapes moving past me. I would find my children. I would.

And then I did. I spotted the silhouettes that unmistakably belonged to me: a taller one and a shorter one, moving slowly together in the deep gloaming, holding hands.

Interlude BETULA

Riverside, California
circa 1979

I watch you as you stand with a metal basin in your hands near that spindly tree at the edge of a dust-choked field, and your pause is long, deliberate before you finally tilt the basin and pour the water into the dry earth bowl around the birch. You have come not with a hose or a watering can, not with a proper vessel for the job, but with an old-fashioned basin for washing of hands, and as the thin stream hits the dirt and sends up a small eruption of dust, I can see already that you will fail. As the water disappears into the earth, you continue to stand in your housedress, looking at the withered tree, which is hardly taller than you and no bigger around than your forearm, and I understand that there is meaning in your standing. You are a tragic heroine, troubled and doomed in a dark Dostoevskian way, though no Dostoevsky character was ever in your particular circumstances—uprooted from your native Russia, and deposited in the parched, ramshackle opulence of citrus country in Southern California.

Of course, since I am only four, I comprehend only the rough outlines of these larger themes, but you are already teaching me what it means to be Russian, what it means to live through symbols, and I recognize that your tragic pose carries a meaning far beyond your simple act of watering a thirsty tree. You've invested your future happiness in this pale, thwarted ghost tree from Russia that doesn't belong here, just as you, my ghost mother from Russia, don't belong here. Do you create this living picture solely for me? Or is it for my American father? His American family? Have you been reduced to speaking through imagery? You, who wrote a PhD dissertation on French literature and taught at a university, now struggle to say and comprehend the simplest things. You will never, in forty years, hear the difference between *sheet* and *shit*.

We stand like this: You in the sun with your basin and tree, in the very center of everything, and I hanging back in the shade of other trees, not quite hidden, not quite revealed. You are turned away from me, but you know I am there, don't you? You speak to me, don't you? Because I am the spectator, the child you brought from Russia, and I am the one who has already begun to betray you, speaking more English than Russian, keenly hearing the difference between *peace* and *piss*, *height* and *hate*. Your standing is a language that I am sure to understand despite my shifting linguistic allegiance, despite my responses to you in English, each word a fresh slap in the face. In your stoic standing you are telling me, sans words, that trees are to be loved and protected, that in them we invest our identities, that they carry within them the places we are from, and that even when they are doomed—or maybe especially when they are doomed—they are important beyond reckoning. My father bought this doomed tree and put it in the ground so you would have Russia just outside the door. Perhaps you know already that the birch is dying. Perhaps you knew from the beginning that California would kill it. And this, too, is part of your message—that we do that which we know will end in heartache, that we relish poignancy, that we seek symbolism in misfortune.

Years later, I will read that birches are a pioneer species that spreads after ice ages, fires, or other ravages, colonizing the land. They live at the extreme northern limits of where trees go, but you are standing with your basin far from any northern limits in the Mediterranean climate of Riverside, California. Birches will not colonize this temperate land. Years later, I will learn that in Russian bathhouses—*banyas*—bathers flagellated themselves with birch branches, and you are flagellating us both, aren't you, in your pathetic stand to insinuate, among California flora, your native vegetation. Years later, I will hear that some of the earliest Slavic writing is preserved on birch bark. Your birch, I will finally see, is your writing on this alien landscape, a ghostly northern specter writ against California sunsets glowing tangerine and plum.

And finally, the picture ends like this: Simply, I tire of watching you, so I turn and run away from you into the other trees, both native and nonnative, that thrive here—palm, navel orange, eucalyptus, mulberry, pepper, floss silk, jacaranda, peach, apricot. I leave you standing with your dying tree, and I don't look back. That is my image for you: a daughter turning her back on her mother, a daughter turning American.

But even now, each time I see the silhouettes of palms against California sky, I am jolted again by the alien inscription they make, spelling out the exotic, the tropical and temperate, the not-me. Even though I spent only three years in my native Russia and the two decades that followed in California, I have yearned for other trees, other places. I live now in a northern clime where birches are native, where snow falls in winter, where the landscape, finally, feels like home. In this land of birches I nurture my own birch, which I planted just outside my front door, and it flourishes, spectral and graceful, but it is a weaker symbol, an echo of you and your birch, an echo of that other time, that other place. And still, this is not Russia, and I do not write these words in Russian. I turn away from you, I disappoint. And though a transplant myself, unlike you I am fluent in the language of my country. Unlike you, I do not need the birch to speak for me.

West Hartford, Connecticut

THE SEASON OF BIRDS AND STONES

The spring after I turned forty, I started master naturalist school, making the forty-mile drive to Goodwin State Forest every Saturday to walk through the woods and learn the words for things. I felt abraded by my life, worn down to inattentiveness and muteness. Three times a week, I commuted an hour north from central Connecticut to western Massachusetts, where I frantically taught four classes, held my obligatory office hour, then raced back south to meet the school bus. On other days, I graded endless essays and did class prep, hauling heaps of papers to the pool for swim practice, to the art league for ceramics. I had been a mother for a decade. I had spent a quarter of my life on children. Master naturalist school felt like an escape, a time and place to have my own life when most of it belonged to others. This feels like a confession. There are things mothers are not supposed to say.

What is a naturalist? The lead instructor, a retired school teacher named Juan, posed this question during the first class. My twenty classmates—most older than me, some by two or three decades—tossed out answers. *Someone who is curious about the natural world. A generalist, not a specialist. A person who observes and appreciates nature.* Juan nodded in encouragement. He told us that the work of a naturalist can be done virtually anywhere, even a street corner. Then he told the story of Margaret Morse Nice, an Ohio housewife who singlehandedly carried out one of the most extensive studies of song sparrows ever conducted in between her mothering and housekeeping duties. *Housewife.* The word rankled. It felt dismissive. I wanted to know more about this woman who had, nearly a century ago, gone outside to be with birds.

We all traipsed into the forest, following Juan, pausing to consider a young yellow birch, *Betula alleghaniensis,* that seemed to be elevated on stilts, its roots appearing to cradle something—only there was nothing in their empty grasp. *What happened here?* Juan wanted to know. These were the kinds of questions naturalists asked. He offered his hypothesis: The birch had originally grown atop a fallen tree that provided nutrients, those elevated roots cradling a nurse log that had since rotted away. My fellow naturalists murmured their appreciation for Juan's divination, but I kept circling what felt like a more urgent question. Who was Margaret Morse Nice? What was her story?

Mothers & Stones

My mother-in-law, Martha Gilman Hamilton, had died nearly three years before I set out to become a master naturalist. Though my husband Doug and I had been married for a dozen years at the time of her death, I had never met her. I knew her only through stories, through words. I knew she was raised in an affluent Los Angeles family, her father a well-known architect, her mother a society lady. Born in 1935, she was the eldest of three and the only girl. Her two younger brothers became architects like their father, but Martha was sent to Wellesley College, where her mother and grandmother had gone before her. She had aspirations to become an architect, but denied the opportunity, she married right out of college and became a foreign service wife, living in Turkey, Nepal, Malta, sometimes Washington, D.C. She directed a house of cooks and nannies and mothered in an exacting and aloof manner.

After the marriage dissolved, she took the children to the wilds of New Mexico—defying the terms of the divorce agreement—where she flipped houses, before house flipping even had a name, using the architectural and interior design skills she picked up from her father. She put her children to work on the properties she bought and fed them easy and inexpensive meals—rubbery liver, ground beef doctored with spices. She was set on finishing the task before her—fledging her six children who ranged in age from preschoolers to high schoolers—as efficiently as possible. She sent her eldest son to a boarding school in Switzerland, her only daughter to Rome. When they reached college age, her three eldest sons went off to Ivies—Harvard, Yale, Penn—and then her daughter went to Wellesley. Just her twin boys remained at home. She sent them on study abroad adventures, one to Japan, the other to Yugoslavia. Finally, they left for college.

Then, she reclaimed her life. She washed her hands of the whole mothering enterprise and maintained only sporadic contact with her children through letters. Her first son to marry selected a wife of whom she did not approve, leading to estrangement; she did not establish a relationship with his three children, which set the tenor for her relations with future grandchildren. By the time my children were born—her eighth and ninth grandchild—she had firmly established herself as uninvolved. And by then, she had become a sculptor and was living in a small village in Mexico, surrounded by her sculptures, pursuing the life that perhaps she felt she had been denied for so long: to be an artist, to live on her own terms. She was inscrutable yet eerily familiar to me: a woman who chose to live out her last days alone with her art, a woman who chose stones over people.

Mothers & Birds

My first foray into learning more about Margaret Morse Nice led me to a book, *Women in the Field: America's Pioneering Women Naturalists,* by Marcia Myers Bonta. In a chapter titled "Margaret Morse Nice, Ethologist of the Song Sparrow," I read that Nice has been called the "founder" of ethology—the study of animal behavior under natural conditions. In the second paragraph, I came upon this: "Often described as only a housewife with four children, she would tartly retort, 'I am *not* a housewife, I am a *trained* zoologist.'"

Mothers & Words

In the feminist classic *Writing a Woman's Life,* Carolyn Gold Heilbrun claims that "there are four ways to write a woman's life." A woman may tell her own story in autobiography, she may tell it in fiction, a biographer may tell her story for her, or "the woman may write her own life in advance of living it, unconsciously, and without recognizing or naming the process." Because the "marriage plot" is the story that historically has been the dominant one available to women, they "have been deprived of the narrative, or the texts, plots, or examples, by which they might assume power over—take control of—their own lives."

Heilbrun was a wife and a mother and a successful academic, teaching for more than three decades at Columbia. When she died in 2003, Vanessa Grigoriadis noted in a *New York Magazine* article: "Heilbrun is one of the mothers—perhaps the mother—of academic feminism, laying the groundwork for women's struggle over the past decades with what they called the 'patriarchy.'"

Heilbrun graduated from Wellesley in 1947, a decade before my mother-in-law Martha. According to Grigoriadis, Heilbrun believed that Wellesley promoted a type of woman who "pursued domestic and volunteer careers with a besotted devotion to ladylike attitudes and the mindless cheer of the lower half of a two-person career—for example, 'We have just moved with our seven children, two dogs, guinea pigs, and the new addition to our family, a large turtle, to an igloo on an ice floe where Dick hopes to study frozen minnows.'"

Swap out a few of the details—six children instead of seven, Turkey or Nepal instead of an ice floe, George instead of Dick—and the story grows eerily familiar.

Stones

I signed up my children for a carving class at the art league. The teacher, an elderly woman named Joan, had been carving stone since before I was born. "My husband of fifty-three years died in February," she told me at the first class. "I miss him so. I love working with the children. They give me something to look forward to each week." She showed me the first sculpture she had ever carved—a sinuous, organic shape, polished smooth. "I carved this forty-eight years ago," she said. "It travels with me to all of my classes." She taught my children how to use rasps, how to shape the stone to their will. It was slow work, their progress nearly imperceptible from one week to the next. Each class, I would pause and watch before leaving to grade essays. Each week, I imagined my own hands shaping those stones.

Mothers & Words

When Doug informed his mother that we were getting married, she sent me a gift: a copy of Charlotte Perkins Gilman's "The Yellow Wallpaper." This may seem an odd nuptial gift—the story of a woman suffering a mental health crisis confined to a room by her physician husband who forbids her from writing and generally controls her life until she suffers a psychotic break—but it was meant as a welcoming gesture. Gilman was a relative of Martha's, appearing on one of the many scrolls of the extensive family tree that reaches all the way back to another literary foremother, Anne Bradstreet, known for being the first published poet of England's North American colonies. Married at sixteen, the mother of eight, Bradstreet writes often of her role as a wife and mother. As a wedding gift, Doug gave me a Nambé bowl (made in New Mexico) with a quote from Bradstreet engraved on the bottom: "I am obnoxious to each carping tongue / Who says my hand a needle better fits." He had grown up with a willful, independent mother who created her own life once her children had grown, and he harbored no resentment, accepting her choices. She had taught him, I think, that women can do what they want; in her willfulness and fierce competence, she raised him to be the kind of man who sees women as the authors of their own stories.

Mothers

I had mined the lives of those who had mothered me—most notably, my own mother and my paternal grandmother—and I was weary of deconstructing their stories, searching them for a blueprint, a way forward. My mother's quest plot was derailed by the marriage plot. She had to give up her quest for knowledge to become a wife, transforming overnight from a confident scholar in the Soviet Union to a reluctant housewife in a foreign country where she didn't speak the language. My American grandmother, in contrast, had no plot to her life—she was still a teenager when she was swept up in the marriage plot, becoming a mother at twenty-one. Did she ever want anything else? Maybe, but she couldn't have said what it was. I'm not sure she ever imagined any other story for herself.

So now I looked to the lives of other mothers, the stories they lived, the stories they told about themselves.

Words

Every Saturday I followed my master naturalist classmates around as they pointed here and there, asking for the words for things, like wide-eyed toddlers. What is this plant? This plant? This tree? This insect? This bird? It seemed miraculous how learning the name for something made it blaze into existence. Once I learned to see sumac, suddenly its red torches sprung out of the tangle of green everywhere I went. The fiddlehead fern, newly indexed, emerged with its distinct scrolls, and the mitten-shaped leaves of the sassafras waved at me everywhere in the forest. One week, we studied plant succession in a powerline corridor, and another, we yanked buckets of water out of a roaring river and peered at aquatic creatures, naming them based on an identification guide. And yet so many of the names trickled out of my leaky brain. I was lucky to retain perhaps one in ten. There were no stories to anchor the names to—nothing to gird them in place. I could remember stories, not disembodied words.

Mothers & Birds

After writing her masterful two-volume study of the song sparrow, Nice tried her hand at writing for a general audience, publishing *The Watcher at the Nest* in 1939. Covering her song sparrow studies but also her studies with cowbirds, warblers, ovenbirds, and mourning doves, as well as her views on conservation, the book was not a commercial success. At the time, it sold 1,006 copies and earned her $206. Still, it's possible to find copies of it in circulation. In a chapter on observing ovenbirds, she shares some of her fascination with the avian world:

> As I watched little mother, I longed to know more of her life. I wished I could have seen the courtship, could have viewed the construction of the quaint little home, and then could have followed the fortunes of the young family after their first venture into the world,

and somehow could have known how they found their way on the incredible journeys to South America and back to these Massachusetts woods. A great admiration for this quiet little bird arose in me, for her self-sufficiency, the simplicity of her life unencumbered by the possessions that overwhelm us human beings. Here she was her own architect, her own provider, bringing up her babies independently of doctors, nurses, books, and even her husband, facing unaided the elements and prowling enemies.

Mothers & Words

Doug has always made sure I had a room of my own—at least figuratively. When the children were babies, he was ever helpful and cheerful, changing diapers, bottle feeding, getting up to calm them in the night. Now that they were older, he walked them to the bus stop in the mornings, drove them to activities. But still, he was the one with a nine-to-five office job, which meant he was unavailable much of the day. And I was the one with an amorphous job that allowed me to be with the children, requiring my presence in a classroom twelve hours a week but otherwise seeping into every crevice of my life, filling my waking hours. My Saturdays were a gift, a jewel gleaming at the end of each long week. Every Saturday, as I pulled out of the driveway to go to master naturalist school, Doug would have the children in the yard pruning shrubs, planting flowers. He continued to give me that room of my own in the ways that he could—even when that room turned out to be a forest forty miles away.

Mothers & Birds

Despite *The Watcher at the Nest* garnering little public attention, Nice undertook the writing of her autobiography, *Research Is a Passion with Me,* which she did not see published in her lifetime. It finally appeared in 1979, five years after her death.

In the early chapters, she describes a relatively happy childhood in a large family in Amherst, Massachusetts. Born in 1883, the fourth of seven children, Nice showed an early interest in the natural world and learned the names of plants from her mother, who studied botany at Mount Holyoke Female Seminary (before it became a college). Nice's most prized possessions were books on bird identification. "In my teens, however, I often felt depressed," she writes, adding:

> Our parents were old-fashioned and over-protective; my mother perpetuated the attitudes of her parents, while my father was determined to spare us the struggles of his own childhood. They did not believe that their daughters should prepare themselves for professions. To be a "perfect housekeeper and homemaker" was the ideal held before us and how dreary it did seem . . . ! We three girls all wished we had been boys, since boys had far more freedom than girls did to explore the world and to choose exciting careers.

What was most galling, Nice reports, was the family rule that the girls were not allowed to walk in the woods or fields without a brother. "Our suggestion that we protect ourselves with a revolver met with strong disapprobation." Still, during her junior year of college at Mount Holyoke, she got both a rifle and a revolver, and she often went armed into the countryside by herself.

Mothers & Words

Over a dozen years, Martha and I exchanged occasional letters—a stiff correspondence conducted in impeccable cursive. I always addressed her as Mrs. Hamilton, my elder, and even her name felt distant and aloof, a further remove—for it was neither her maiden name nor her first married name and the name of her children, but rather the name of her third husband. *Dear Mrs. Hamilton,* I began, though I no longer remember what I wrote to her. She wrote back of the books she'd read, of her small town in Mexico, of her Great Danes, of her gardening successes and failures. Her tone was breezy and detached; it was a correspondence of small talk.

"The excitement in our compound, this week, is swirling around house-wren's nest in an Aztec mask hung on house-wall across from my apt.," she wrote on June 25, 2001, a year after Doug and I were married. "Yesterday, for first time, I could hear babies chirping when fed. Previously, there were parents' marvelous songs and a special curse-sound when our cat is in view. The parents flit into/out the eye-holes and top of head and sometimes perch, momentarily, on ear-ornaments. As long as light holds, they are collecting insects for the babies!"

Mothers & Words

"What matters is that lives do not serve as models; only stories do that," writes Heilbrun in *Writing a Woman's Life*. She continues:

> And it is a hard thing to make up stories to live by. We can only retell and live by the stories we have read or heard. We live our lives through texts. They may be read, or chanted, or experienced electronically, or come to us, like the murmurings of our mothers, telling us what conventions demand. Whatever their form or medium, these stories have formed us all; they are what we must use to make new fictions, new narratives.

In *A Room of One's Own*, Virginia Woolf, one of Heilbrun's literary mothers, writes, "For we think back through our mothers if we are women." And also: "For books continue each other, in spite of our habit of judging them separately." And Heilbrun adds (nearly six decades later), "We tell ourselves stories of our past, make fictions or stories of it, and these narrations *become* the past, the only part of our lives that is not submerged."

In other words, all that remains of our past is words. In other words, all that remains of *us* is words. But are words enough?

Stones

At home, the children shaped other stones. The rock tumbler was always groaning in the basement, grinding away the sharp edges of rocks found on hikes and travels. The children's rock collections spilled out of their plastic containers into multiple shoeboxes. When doing laundry, I often found rocks squirreled away in pockets. On our walks up the street, my son always took a single rock from a meticulously landscaped yard where the plants were nestled in iridescent gravel. Did those neighbors notice that their gravel disappeared, piece by piece, over weeks, months, into the greedy fist of my boy? Sometimes, despite my careful pocket searches, a vigilante rock made it through the wash and then clattered in the dryer, tumbling among the clothes. This endless shaping and moving of rocks seemed like the elemental work of being human—for hadn't we always picked up rocks, exerted our will on them? Wasn't a rock one of the most substantial and satisfying gifts offered up to us by the earth?

Mothers & Stones

We have a binder containing slides and black-and-white photographs of Martha's sculptures. A piece called *Frederick's Ferret* features an inquisitive, sleek animal peering over the top of a human head. It is, according to a typewritten inventory list, made of varied hue soapstone. Most of Martha's pieces are made of soapstone in a range of colors. Her whimsical forms have titles like *Transcendent Koi, Ancient Aerobics, Two Patriarchs Harmonizing Their Minds,* and *Generic Dreamgirl.*

"My deep commitment is to create useful and intelligent art. Specifically, I intend beauty and humor pointed toward healing," she writes in her artist's statement. "Collectors who live with my sculpture say they find solace in it: healing, quieting. Stroking the seductive silky stone is fulfilling, and it's an aid to meditation." The stones, she writes, tell her what they want to be. "The sculpture shapes come from persistent dreams and from the stone's suggestion," she continues. "The subject figures affirm—with energy and joy—the strength of our human capacity for lust, commitment, spirituality." But I don't see this in her works. They are too abstract for me. I see that she is trying to say something, but I don't know what it is.

Birds

On the Saturday devoted to birds, the naturalists carried binoculars into the woods. I peered at the darting asterisks in treetops, but I saw little. I've never had the patience to look through microscopes, binoculars, telescopes, loupes, magnifying glasses—the images come at me frenetic and blurry. Maybe it's because I wear glasses, and I don't want to add more lenses in front of my eyes, which often seem to obstruct more than they clarify. I listened to Juan talk about birds and tried to take good notes. The towhee, I learned, sings, "Drink your tea!" and the barn owl asks, "Who cooks for you?" In my notebook, I dutifully listed the three types of swallows found in Connecticut, the characteristics of the grackle. But at some point, I lost interest in the birds, in the naming of them, in the elusiveness of their lives in treetops. Instead, I wrote wayward questions. *What is more amazing—a feather or an eye?*

Mothers & Birds

In one exuberant section of *Research Is a Passion with Me,* Nice describes going on a tump-line camping trip with her fifteen-year-old younger brother Ted: "He had sewed food bags on the sewing machine; he had experimented with drying corn and blackberries; he planned, assembled, and rejected until at last all was ready. We were to carry house, blankets, kitchen, wardrobes, and larder on our backs by means of tump-lines—broad leather straps over the forehead, the pack resting on the small of the back." They covered ninety miles in two weeks, and Nice had the time of her life. "We had been brought near the primal sources of life," she writes. "This experience might be thought of as a parable of life; a journey, stripped down to essentials and involving struggle and hardship, to see and to love some of the wonder of the world."

Enrolling in graduate school, Nice continued her studies, despite her parents' wishes that she become a "daughter-at-home." She writes:

> My intention on going to Clark University had been to get an M.A. on "The Food of the Bobwhite." I was so happy there that I decided to use this subject for a Ph.D. thesis; this in spite of strong family opposition, for my parents urged me unceasingly to return again and be a daughter-at-home. In my second year I continued my feeding tests . . . , and for the early summer of 1909 I had planned to carry out a large series of such tests with baby Bobwhites at the State Hatchery at nearby Sutton. In August there was to be a canoe trip with Ted in "really wild country."

What happened next puzzled me so much that I reread the section three times. "These plans were changed. Instead of raising Bobwhites, I was married; instead of working for a Ph.D., I kept house."

Her new husband was a fellow graduate student, Leonard Blaine Nice, who was, by all accounts, a wonderful man. Still, her life radically changed course. "Sometimes I rather regretted that I had not gone ahead and obtained this degree [her PhD], as we stayed in Worcester for two more years until Blaine got his Ph.D.," she adds. "But no one had ever encouraged me to study for a doctor's degree; all the propaganda had been against it. My parents were more than happy to have me give up thoughts of a career and take up home-making, and in every way they helped us in this new venture."

Mothers & Words

In one letter, Martha wrote to tell me about what she was reading: "Just finished second slow, leisurely reading of *The Ambassadors* by Henry James . . . . such a deep pleasure, how could I have waited so long . . . ? Maybe, to be the right age, myself, to understand and sympathize with Strether. He seems to reflect a lot of my Grandmother's influence/training on me."

I was in graduate school at this time, and I started sending her some of my writing. After reading an essay that I had written about trees, she responded: "Marvelously thoughtful and stimulating! I'm deeply concerned by your suggestion there may not be trees after death. I've been hoping and counting on pines, palms, buddlia and pachysandra as well as deer, ground hogs, insects and jays!"

Birds & Words

Master naturalist school required each student to conduct an independent research project. One classmate was studying salamanders in a vernal pool. Another was researching the history of local colliers and learning how to make a charcoal mound, a replica of which he planned to erect in the forest for educational purposes. I had no research project in mind, but I regularly walked with my children to a nearby wetland area that teemed with red-winged blackbirds.

One afternoon, sitting on a bench while my children sent cattail fluff sailing on the wind, I was struck with a vague fancy that I would become the Margaret Morse Nice of red-winged blackbirds. Or at least I would do my research project on the birds, since here they were, right in front of me.

The next time we came, I brought a notebook and sat down at the edge of the cattail-choked pond to begin my observations. I watched the loud, boastful males flitting through the vegetation, crying *conk-ra-lee!* Or perhaps *chip-chiree!* Or *oak-la-ree!* I watched the occasional drab female emerge briefly from the cattails, then merge back into the camouflage. If Nice could devote years of her life to song sparrows, then surely I could devote a few weeks to red-winged blackbirds. While the idea of studying birds appealed to me, I found that I could muster no interest in gathering real data: counting the birds, telling them apart, recording their calls and movements, counting how many times they landed in various locations, discerning which ones seemed to be mated pairs. Showy and pompous, the males darted and preened and cried *irk-a-chee!* I watched them but recorded nothing in my notebook.

Birds & Words

I came across an old book, *Redwings*, by Robert W. Nero, published by the Smithsonian Institution Press in 1984. Here, at last, I would learn something about the birds that darted among the grasses and cattails at the pond. But most of the book turned out to be dull, nearly unreadable, detailing endless observations of bird behavior. Only a few sections held my interest. For example, what Nero had to say about the red-winged blackbird's call:

> Anyone who has been near a marsh in spring has heard male Red-winged Blackbirds, but describing their song is another matter. I like what Arthur Allen . . . noted in 1914: "The greatest difficulty lies in the selection of words, letters, or symbols that will convey a sound similar to that uttered by the bird." He used *con-cur-ee, kong-quer-ree,* and *gur-gel-lee* as common renditions of the basic or primary song. In my work with Redwings I chose *oak-a-lee* or *oak-a-ree* as

> most descriptive (leaving *aujourd'hui* for Canada's French-speaking bird watchers). Ardythe McMaster, a Winnipeg teacher, told me that when she was young her mother always referred to the song as *Purple-tea!*

Sitting at the pond, I listened to birds trilling their signature calls and tried to discern their true utterances. *Konk-la-ree! Honk-a-ree! Tur-a-lee! Kor-a-lee! Get-me-tea! Come-to-me!*

Mothers

In 1913 Nice, along with her growing family, relocated to Norman, Oklahoma, where her husband got an appointment teaching at the university. Nice, settling down to keep house, found her early years of motherhood were nothing short of maddening:

> In the fall of 1918, with four children aged six months to eight years, in what seemed to be cramped quarters, no one enjoying housework, and much of the time without even a college girl to come in an hour a day to wash the dishes, with no means of transportation but our own legs and the baby carriage, and no free Sunday afternoon for tramps to the river, I was truly frustrated. I resented that implication that my husband and the children had brains, and I had none. He taught; they studied; I did housework.

Mothers & Words

Two months after the birth of our daughter, Martha wrote to us: "Congratulations to the three of you. I'm happy for your future, as first-born has fewer complications and most excitement." She also reported on her health. "My heart health is back to 120 over 80 and I feel fine," she wrote. "Gout is a major surprise to me, and hope I haven't genetically shared it. In any case, it didn't manifest until I'm 69, so you all have many healthy years ahead."

Several months later, after I sent her a photo of the baby, she wrote to say our daughter's "lip-line is gorgeous, absolutely phenomenal, and she seems happy & sturdy. Congratulations on a stage excellently accomplished. Your marvelous quality writing-paper always impresses me."

Birds & Words

In *Redwings*, Nero tries to describe female red-winged blackbird vocalizations:

> The song itself? Well, it's not a version of *"oak-a-lee"* or anything close to the male rendition. Female song consists rather of a series of chattering, scolding tones rendered in my earliest field notes as *"spit-a-chew-chew-chew."* Beginning with a short rasping sound, the female song then goes off into a series of high, shrill, and rapid notes, slowing and descending at the end. Don't, for heaven's sake, read *"spit-a-chew-chew"*; instead, purse your lips and give a short chirping sound, staccato. It's the best I can do.

Other ornithologists—also men—have described the song as "female chatter" that is "harsh and rasping." It's the best they can do.

Words

"Before a woman can write exactly as she wishes to write, she has many difficulties to face," Woolf writes in "Women and Fiction," an essay that she would fold into *A Room of One's Own*. "To begin with, there is the technical difficulty—that the very form of the sentence does not fit her. It is a sentence made by men; it is too loose, too heavy, too pompous for a woman's use." A woman must take on the task of "altering and adapting the current sentence until she writes one that takes the natural shape of her thought without crushing or distorting it." Heilbrun reiterates this idea over half a century later: "How can women create stories of women's lives if they have only male language with which to do it?"

Birds & Words

A long, long time ago, sparrow, swallow, and blackbird started boasting. "I can fly as high as the tops of the trees," said sparrow. "I can fly as high as the clouds," countered swallow. "Oh, really? Well, I can fly as high as the sun," replied blackbird, the most prideful of all birds. So, the birds decided to have a contest. Little sparrow went first, flying with all his might up, up, up, but he barely cleared the top of the tallest tree before he grew exhausted and came back to Earth. Next, swallow made his attempt. He flapped and flapped his wings and flew much higher than sparrow, but nowhere near the sun.

I was back at the red-winged blackbird pond with my children, and I had finally written something in my notebook. But this fanciful fairy tale hardly counted as fieldwork, I thought, as I watched my children carrying lances made of cattails.

Mothers & Words

After I sent Martha a copy of *Local Wonders* by Ted Kooser—with whom I was studying in my graduate program—she wrote to express her appreciation.

> Last night I found the book of Ted Kooser's and am loving it to extent I wish I'd written it. So far, it's right up there with Edward Abbey's *Desert Solitaire,* except Kooser does people much better.
>
> Excitement down here is limited to "cho-cho" devastation (small grasshoppers in hordes) & where my Dane's overnite digging will be. Have you ever heard of a Gt. Dane digging for sport? We're (2 mornings' weekly helper & I) laying new sod over all the bare soil that attracts her attention. Her front nails are worn to quick. . . . I keep hoping it's simple puppyishness as she does so many other puppy tricks: biting hoses into parts; dragging everything of mine outside, including my hard leather glasses' case! She'd already been bred when she was given to me; they told me she was *two;* how long will this go on, do you think?
>
> Boston doctors are thinking my problems are temporary & reversible: nerve-groups are pinched by neck vertebras, rather than any damage to my spinal column itself. Hurrah! except they want another test.
>
> Back to our "cho-cho"s: slightly more interesting than health. They denuded a clump of ash-trees of leaves; my 4-y-old honeysuckle is definitely killed, as are most jasmines & all the ornamental citrus shrubs. I've even seen them on eucalyptus and lemons, so they'll excuse the *taste* of leaves. In this season, they're mating; so I can count 200 gone from next year's crop for every pair I squish!
>
> Affectionately yours,
> Martha Hamilton

Mothers & Words

I went to college with the intention of becoming a journalist and got my first newspaper job when I was nineteen. But after four years working at daily newspapers, telling other people's stories, skimming the surface of their lives in the most superficial manner, I was worn thin, exhausted. By then, I had dropped out of college, and when I finally went back, I was looking for another path. Edging my way back into academic life, I signed up for just one course: a survey of British literature. I enjoyed it enough that at the end of the first semester, I enrolled for the second half of the sequence. I had taken a yearlong survey of British literature in high school, and much of the content was the same—a whirlwind tour from *Beowulf* through the present—but when I reached the twentieth century in the college sequence, I was assigned a novel by Virginia Woolf, a writer I'd never read before. When I first opened the pages of *To the Lighthouse*, I felt (in Emily Dickinson's words) "as if the top of my head were taken off." Here, at last, was an invitation into a world of letters, a place for me. Here, in the characters of Mrs. Ramsay and Lily Briscoe, were a mother and a female artist, rendered exquisitely. They lived before my very eyes. Here was a writer who wrote about our internal lives—the great but mostly silent battles that are fought in our minds, every single day. Here was a woman who understood that the small epiphanies of everyday life—"moments of being"—are our greatest gifts, and that perhaps a life is no more than a string of these moments like pearls shining out of the darkness of the "nondescript cotton wool" that makes up most of our quotidian existence. Here were the sentences that crept sinuously, associatively across pages, giving shape to consciousness—female consciousness. Here was an invitation meant just for me: Come tell your story.

When I first read the novel, in my early twenties, its message seemed simple enough: One could be a mother like Mrs. Ramsay, giving away all of her energies to her husband and children, or one could be an artist like the spinster Lily Briscoe, who hoarded her creativity and fought against the crushing weight of the patriarchy to create her art. Unmarried and childless, I admired the clarity of the choice presented to me. But of course, it was not as simple as

I imagined. The great struggle of my thirties would be to embrace Mrs. Ramsay and Lily Briscoe both, to learn how to be a mother *and* an artist.

Mothers & Words

When my daughter first learned to speak, she was voracious, demanding words, more words. I took to carrying a notebook and recording every word she said. At eighteen months of age, she could say 352 words—or at least that was how many I managed to write down. Indexing the world with her little pointer finger, she cataloged and named everything. Car, dog, tree, mom, rock. In her mouth she carried words, in her fists she carried rocks. She was equally tethered to both worlds—the cerebral, the corporeal. It had been so long since I had written anything substantial that the list I made of her words felt like my own accomplishment. My creative work was now this child, her acquisition of language my achievement, her expression very nearly my own.

Mothers & Words

When Nice's children were very young, she, too, counted the words they knew. But she went a step further: She undertook a scientific study of the subject. "It was the challenge of the problem—how did the child acquire his language?" she wrote in her autobiography. "The more I observed and recorded and the more I worked over my results, the more questions presented themselves. My small subjects were always with me and each showed a different picture." She published a few papers on the subject—"The Speech Development of a Child from Eighteen Months to Six Years," "Ambidexterity and Delayed Speech Development," "The Speech of a Left-Handed Child," "A Child That Would Not Talk"—but her lack of a PhD and professional status stymied her from really breaking into the field.

Birds & Words

Finally, it was blackbird's turn. He took off and began to fly. Up and up he flew, farther and farther. He flew past the treetops, he flew past the clouds, he flew until he became a speck and then disappeared completely from view of the other birds, who were watching from a perch on a tree branch. He grew exhausted, but he kept flying, because in addition to being boastful, he was also very determined. He thought his little heart might explode in his chest, his wings might seize with cramps, but he kept flying. And finally, the sun came into view. It grew bigger and bigger, until he was blinded by its light, kissed by its heat, but he just kept going. He flew and flew until he began to feel an unpleasant heat on his wings and shoulders, and then a smoldering sensation. The next thing he knew, he was on fire! Quickly, he stopped flapping and began to plummet toward the ground. Luckily, the wind put the fire out, and his wings and shoulders were only singed, now displaying the markings of the sun: red and yellow. When he finally returned, exhausted, the other birds cheered enthusiastically, for indeed blackbird was the highest flier among them. And to this day, blackbird—now red-winged blackbird—wears the distinctive red and yellow epaulets that mark his achievement.

"And what happened next?" my children wanted to know, eager for more story. We were back at the pond, and I had read my story out loud.

"And then red-winged blackbird settled into a quiet life at the pond and lived happily ever after. And do you know what red-winged blackbird says?"

"O-bugger-dee!"

"Oh, look at me!" I replied. "Because red-winged blackbird wants everyone to admire him. He flew too close to the sun and was made beautiful by it."

Mothers

Virginia Woolf was born in 1882, the year before Margaret Morse Nice. They were contemporaries, but their lives were radically different. Woolf lived in England, she wasn't offered the opportunity to receive a college education, and she had no children. Nice was an American, college educated, a mother. Woolf was interested in words, Nice in birds. Still, as contemporaries, they speak to one another, and they speak to me now of an era that seems both a long time ago and just yesterday. As Woolf reminds us in *A Room of One's*

Own, it was only after 1880 that a married woman was allowed to possess property in England, and it was not until 1919 (in the United States, 1920)—when Woolf and Nice were already well into their thirties—that a woman could vote.

And it was in 1919, at the age of thirty-six, that Nice began what would become her life's work: She turned her attention to birds. She started taking one day a month for herself to get to know the birds of Oklahoma. "It is an inspiring experience to have a day for wandering—to be free and alone with nature for a whole long day; to feel unhurried; to be able to search carefully for birds, to be unmolested by considerations for other people." With her husband's help, she meticulously conducted a bird census of Oklahoma.

When his job took the family to Columbus, Ohio, in 1928, Nice began her in-depth study of the song sparrow, the work for which she would become most famous. "In child care, male song sparrows are exemplary," she writes, one of thousands of observations she made about the birds. "They are the sole incubators of the eggs, and after the nestlings hatch, they help care for the young."

According to Bonta, Blaine Nice "was the most amiable of men. He encouraged her in all she attempted, took care of the girls when she was pursuing research, and was always happy to finance her work."

Mothers & Words

Around the time our daughter was born, Doug's eldest brother sent Martha a book of questions with blank spaces for her to write down her life story for his children. *A Grandparent's Book,* it was called, and she went through it, writing her answers to the prompts, in some cases adding extra pages when she ran out of room, and in others completely ignoring questions that she had no interest in answering. Eventually, copies of the book were made for all of the siblings, and I finally started reading it that spring I was going to master naturalist school.

As I expected, her accounts of her early life speak of privilege and wealth. In one house in which her family lived, she describes "a bedroom for the maids." In another section on holiday traditions, she writes, "Gilman family holidays were based on tradition of maids in the kitchen cooking elegantly." She describes horseback riding in beautiful, unspoiled Southern California. "Our father had been in the mounted cavalry in the previous war and he'd remained horse-fond & much later began a Morgan Horse Stud called Green Valley. His great stallion was Tom Boy, so sweet Daddy rode him in several Rose Parades."

Her architect father eventually built his family a custom home on their forty-four-acre estate "of wild-natural to splendidly-groomed and kept natural-looking gardens and wilds at almost end of canyon toward ocean." As a young woman, she was "presented to LA Society by the grande dames, called 'Las Madrinas,' at a ball for which I can still remember my father's pride." The photos I have seen confirm my image of a poised, attractive young woman. But then I come to questions and answers that seem to belie my understanding of her.

Were you a healthy new-born baby?
My mother didn't nurse me, or later, her 2 sons. I think it wasn't customary at that time. I never felt cuddled by her.

What are your thoughts about your mother?
My mother was socially expert and athletic, both. I was neither.

What are your thoughts about your father?
My father was a madly successful architect because he really enjoyed people and carefully listened to what his clients thought they wanted. Then he created for their genuine needs.

Do you look more like your mother or your father?
Much more like my father, unfortunately: dark, curly hair, knocked knees, wild eyebrow growth, dark teeth.

Mothers & Words

A month after the birth of our son, Martha wrote to congratulate us. "I am thrilled beyond adequately communicating! We have two 2-daughter families already, & those parents seem to have decided against more children. Two daughters, alone, is my nightmare vision for jealousy/rivalry rather than loving friendships and companionship thru life. I found, also, that boys are sooo much more fun to parent."

Mothers & Words

In *Research Is a Passion with Me,* Nice relates an encounter she had while living in Oklahoma: "It was a rich experience to meet and talk with Charlotte Perkins Stetson Gilman who came to the University at the invitation of President William Bizzell. She gave an impressive lecture on 'The Fundamental Falsity of Freud,' saying that he had 'blackened the face of America.' 'Sex is not the life force,' she said. 'It is only part of life. It is not essential to individual life but to the race.'" Nice calls Gilman "a remarkable woman, brilliant and original, a clear and logical thinker in many fields," but concludes: "Yet, sadly enough, it seems as if she had been a voice crying in the wilderness, for now she appears to be forgotten."

Nice was writing her autobiography in the early seventies, just as the second-wave feminists were rediscovering the work of Gilman and many other women. Gilman, I would warrant, is no longer forgotten.

Mothers & Words

What did you want to be or do when you were finished with high school?

That wasn't a question in my family. I was to graduate from Wellesley before any other life-stage was thinkable or permissible!

Wellesley College was life-goal for me of my gram '88 and my mother '24, as I relied on my daughter (again '88?) to go, and I hope my granddaughters will go, too!

What do you remember best?

My parents packaged and sent me over by nite-plane, florists' boxes of cymbidium sprays from my father's plants under lath-roof above the corral at Wildacres. They were treasures in themselves, for their beauty, and balm for my homesickness! (Never heard of another college-girl receiving sprays of orchids!)

Were you involved in any extra-curricular activities?

Extracurricular for me was dating at all the schools & towns I wanted to visit; trying to keep sane in such extraordinarily different circumstances from my life around LA. It was far & away most extreme culture shock of my life.

Were you a member of any clubs?
Can't imagine any Wellesley club wanting to take me.

Mothers & Words

After suffering a breakdown, after enduring a divorce that was excoriated in the newspapers, after sending her young daughter to live with her ex-husband and his new wife (who happened to be her good friend), Charlotte Perkins Gilman fashioned a writing and speaking career for herself as she rode the lecture circuit, spending many years "at large" with no permanent address. In *Women and Economics*, she writes, "We are the only animal species in which the female depends on the male for food, the only animal species in which the sex-relation is also an economic relation," proclaiming that only economic independence would emancipate women. She considered women's suffrage "such a foregone conclusion that I can't get all excited over it"—though she was sixty before she could vote. In the utopian novel *Herland*, she imagined a world with no men, where women reproduced via parthenogenesis and the institution of motherhood was radically recast such that women mothered all children as a collective responsibility. For the first part of her career, she went by Charlotte Perkins Stetson, her first married name. The year she turned forty, she married George Houghton Gilman (who happened to be her cousin), and then took the last name by which she is still known today. Due to this proliferation of names, her biographer, Cynthia J. Davis, calls her simply Charlotte.

In her lifetime, Gilman was attacked for being "an unnatural mother," among many other faults. In recent years, following her recovery by feminists, she's been criticized for her ethnocentrism, racism, nationalism, and other vices. She was—as we all are—complicated and contradictory. Davis writes that Gilman "claims to have lived her life according to a plot she had carefully scripted." Whether that plot was really conceived in advance or rather constructed in hindsight, it gave her mastery over her own story. The title of her autobiography, *The Living of Charlotte Perkins Gilman*, stresses the active agency that she strived to maintain over her life. Her life was not something that happened to her, but rather her living was something she actively did.

Birds & Words

Other stories came to me at the pond. In one version, the red-winged blackbird's epaulets denote his status as a decorated military veteran, the bravest of the avian world. In another, the birds started out brilliantly colored, red-orange-yellow all over, as beautiful and alluring as the Russian *zhar-ptitsa*, or Firebird, but they developed a propensity for lying, and each time they told a lie, a small patch of pitch black developed on their plumage, and slowly their colors were obscured until only the dabs of red-orange-yellow remained on their shoulders. In another story, the blackbirds of the New World decided to distinguish themselves from their cousins, the blackbirds of the Old World, by getting matching tattoos. Many stories I started writing but never finished. Some days, I tried to render exactly the sounds the birds made as they chattered, scolded, trilled, tweeted, chirruped, chittered, chirred, trilled, cheeped—but all words, all possible renderings, were inexact approximations of what they actually said.

Mothers & Words

How old were you when you met my grandfather/grandmother?
I think I was 13 and George would have been two years older.

What attracted you to each other?
I was attracted because he didn't talk a lot, but what he said made very good sense. I can't answer the reverse.

How long did you know each other before you discussed marriage?
Think I must have been around 19, but don't much remember, except I was eager to see the world with him!

How many houses or apartments did you live in?
It's interesting to add them up: eight different places on three continents before we split, I'm guessing.

What surprised you about my grandfather/grandmother after you married?

Your grandfather was able for only one ejaculation per night!

Mothers & Stones

A year earlier, on a trip to Iceland, as we walked on the black sand beach at Vik, my daughter, who was then nine, walked into the surf and was swept up and away from me, just for a moment, until I grabbed her and yanked her back again, and then we kept walking. I picked up an oblong black stone that had been worried smooth by the sea, and I put it in my coat pocket where I rubbed it, over and over. Later, as we dried out and ate lamb stew at a café, I imagined what would have happened if I hadn't snatched my daughter back from the sea, and I worked the stone, over and over, in my palm. To this day, I carry that black worry-stone from Iceland in the pocket of my coat. To this day, my fingers rub, rub, rub, continuing the work of the sea.

Mothers & Stones

When her twins were teenagers and her other children had left home, Martha placed a personal ad in *The New York Review of Books*, which eventually led her to her second and then her third husband. Of her second marriage, she writes: "Stu, delightful and kindly to us all, was impotent; so marriage was annulled." And it was this failed marriage, she adds, that led to her sculpting: "Realized that my sexual frustration needed something hard & physical for me to keep calm and sane. A couple of my untaught pieces expressed something to others, as they sold in Boise, ID and in Ajijic, Jalisco." It was only after she married Louis that she sought formal training in sculpture, studying with Morse Clary, a disciple of Philip McCracken. Despite remaining married, Martha lived apart from Louis for most of their marriage, moving around the country—Portland, Boise, New York, Philadelphia—while her husband seemed to stay put on his ranch in Washington state. After she headed to Mexico, her marriage was reduced to one of the many correspondences that she kept up with far-flung acquaintances.

Mothers & Words

What are the best gifts you've ever received?
My children.

Do you believe in God?
Sorta.

What holiday traditions do you hope I give to my own children?
Real celebration, like real prayer, I think, should be internal, unvocalized, and not depending on decorations, foods, or people making trips to be together.

Whom do you love? What do you love?
Louis and my children. I love the world, with trees and animals foremost. Beautiful buildings, bird-songs and good food are important too, and BOOKS!

What talents or abilities have you tried to develop?
My sculpting.

What are your other interests?
Solitude and quiet and preparing my mind.

Mothers & Birds

Besides undertaking her song sparrow study, something else momentous happened to Nice and her family in 1928 that gets only the briefest mention in her autobiography. "A great sorrow came to us that winter in the loss of our daughter, Eleanor, a beautiful courageous child of nine years," she writes. "In her memory we gave a set of 50 children's books to the State University Hospital in Columbus and 100 children's books to the Public Library in Norman." By the next paragraph, though, Nice is back to birds, and, in fact, by March, she's banding her first song sparrow and embarking on her life's great work. For the next eight years, she will devote herself to song sparrows, experiencing great "expectation and frustration, triumph and failure."

I kept expecting her to return to her loss, to devote more words to grieving her daughter, but that's not the kind of story she's telling. It's *research* that's a passion with her, after all—or at least that's the plot she's adopted. Her most impassioned writing comes when she's describing her work, as in this entry from Jan. 29, 1933:

> I am now spending *all* my available energies on Song Sparrows—an hour or so outdoors with them in the morning; the rest of the day on writing, except for what has to go for sleeping, eating, getting breakfast and lunch and a little more house work. (Our daughters prepare dinner and wash all the dishes.) I write all morning after coming in, rest perhaps an hour after lunch and then write again all afternoon. In the evening I am now going through all the great Song Sparrow note books, having reached No. XII with ten more to go. I'm finding many important items.

In reading her pages upon pages of exuberant bird words, one might even suppose that she threw herself into the song sparrow project as a kind of grieving.

Mothers & Words

A section of *A Grandparent's Book* on work and career is largely blank. Martha writes of working as a technical writer briefly after her marriage before her first child was born. Then she adds: "Haven't enough courage to be a principal. Have always assisted someone: an autistic child; an elderly woman; a working mother needing after-school care for 2; cleaning good houses; writers needing grammar assistance; office-temps for secretarial help."

I felt disappointed in her for settling for the supporting role. Her series of sporadic, strung-together jobs gave her no sense of purpose, no greater narrative arc. Her story lacks plot.

Mothers & Words

What does it say about me that I am more interested in the woman who studied birds than the birds she studied? That I am more interested in my own stories about red-winged blackbirds than their actual lives? Could I be more interested in my stories about my children than my actual children? What does it say about me that my words become more valuable than the experiences they describe? Or is it just that the words are the only way I have of holding onto experiences, onto people? If I remake my children out of words, I can keep them forever, just as they are. If I build myself out of words, I will continue to exist.

For all of my growing up years, my own mother had believed that books were more important than people, that only art could save you in the end. And even though years later, after she had forged an academic career for herself in the United States, after she had retired, she recanted this view, writing, "It took almost my entire life to come to the conclusion that people are more important and necessary than books are," perhaps I can never supplant my earliest belief that the story is always truer, more vivid, more essential than the lived experience. Perhaps I will never fully let go of the belief that there is nothing more important than art.

Mothers & Words

In the "family lore" section of the book, Martha describes what she knows of her grandparents, including the following story about her paternal grandmother:

> I can't guess where Lucy Truesdell came from, as she wasn't discussed at all until I was 21. I was then told that she had been at Oberlin Conservatory studying her music when her roommate/best-friend introduced her to my grandfather. They married & had 2 sons. The day my father, the elder son, called to say he had passed his tests for Architecture degree, she shot herself in the head with her shotgun. Even sadder, her younger son, my Uncle Lucius, was the one who discovered her body.

She provides no further commentary on this event.

Birds & Words

In another section of *Redwings,* Nero describes the behavior of a particular female that leaves male A to breed with male B. "Let's not call her a fickle female," Nero moralizes. "Let's say instead that she found the habitat in B's territory more to her liking than the habitat in A's territory." Elsewhere, in discussing females, he uses terms like "promiscuity" and "loose behavior." It strikes me, not for the first time, that the stories we tell about other species are really stories about ourselves.

Birds & Words

Pages of my notebook were filled with red-winged blackbird stories. I had certainly spent at least twenty-five hours—the requirement for our research project—at the pond, observing the birds. But I had nothing that looked like fieldnotes. And it struck me, woefully late, that I hadn't told any stories about the females, those drab and dull creatures. I hardly noticed them. Of course, there's the not-insignificant fact that the bird's common name refers to a characteristic of the male, as does its scientific name, *Agelaius phoeniceus,* the epithet meaning "red" in Latin. By this very naming, I was taught what to see: the showy wings of the males. What story would I even tell about the females? That they had given up those ostentatious and garish marks to live their lives largely unobserved? That they had sacrificed a life of adventure to be mothers?

After spending weeks walking through forests and poring over lists of scientific names of species, was this small realization of my own blindness all I had to show for it? I began to wonder why I had gone to master naturalist school in the first place. Was it just to escape from my children? Were my Saturday master naturalist classes merely a vacation from motherhood? Like so many other mothers—including Martha and my own mother—I was an ambivalent mother. During their mothering years, they both recognized there were other plots they could be living, and they both grasped them, in the end, but it took the fledging of their children for them to fully come into their own. I didn't know how not to be an ambivalent mother. The world is full of them. Both the nurturing of children and the nurturing of the self is writ into the human brain, wired into our biology, at cross-purposes. It's easy to say I would give my life to save my child's—take a bullet, run into the path of an oncoming car—but the choices are rarely that obvious. The choices are daily, small, carried out over years.

Mothers & Words

What are you most proud of doing?

Escaping to Mexico. To have found the courage to arrange the trip; to subject dear Louis into sending my sculpture stones from his ranch; to locate correct climate for me, a reasonable rental-house. All of this effort and mental activity gives me reason, I think, to be proud to end my life as I wish to.

What was your most exciting experience?

Becoming fluent in Turkish! Understanding people came first, of course. Then I could express myself with degrees of honorifics and nuances. I could go anywhere and do anything I chose throughout the entire fascinating country. Not being mute was liberating of vast dimensions, for five wonderful years. In Nepal there were too many language groups to attempt any; on Malta, many people spoke English. In Turkey I could interact with guests, hosts, people sitting nearby on trains, in restaurants. Of course, I was proud of my fluency, as many Americans don't bother to learn. Was so fluent I could even tell slightly risqué stories at parties and be entertaining.

For me, "was" isn't appropriate tense. My happiest living is day-to-day down here in Morelia. Climate is within extremes of So Cal, while I was a child, so with my a-c for sleeping, I don't fear any seasons. The altitude agrees with me, 7,000+-, so I can walk for pleasure . . . with my neighbor's old Golden Retriever 3x-weekly for about an hour . . . or alone to visit acquaintances, or get cash from the bank, or on errands to Santa Maria Village. I don't have TV, phone, or radio so nothing intrudes. I've completed my responsibilities to everyone.

Mothers & Words

In the final pages of her autobiography, Nice writes:

> It is true that I deplore much in the present situation in the world—basically due to overcrowding—yet for many of the features of civilization I am profoundly thankful: for instance, the comparative freedom of women, the advances in medical science, the availability

> of classical music over FM radio, the great improvements in photographic techniques, paperback books printed in America, electric refrigerators, electric and gas stoves, frozen foods, and for transportation—the convenience of the automobile, and the marvellous experience of flying over the earth.

She and Blaine both lived to be ninety, dying a few months apart. "She had had a wonderfully satisfying life as a wife and mother, but she had managed to combine it with a career she designed for herself," Bonta writes at the conclusion of her chapter-long biography of Nice. She got her marriage plot and quest plot both—a happy ending. A life to emulate.

Yet I wonder if the "conventional" parts of Nice's life—falling in love, losing a child—appear in her writing in only the most cursory manner because she was resisting the marriage plot even as she lived it. The "housewife" narrative and all that it entailed (both joy and sorrow) did not make her exceptional. In defying the marriage plot—lest it take over her whole narrative—she had to suppress those parts of her life. It makes much of her adult life, from the moment of her marriage, seem oddly affectless. I am convinced that she was a warm and loving wife and mother—but she balks at telling those parts. Her life is not the same thing as the story of her life. In every story she tells about herself, the emphatic subtext is always the same: "I am *not* a housewife, I am a *trained* zoologist."

Mothers & Words

Some of the questions Martha left blank:
Did you win any academic, social or athletic awards or prizes?
What did you like best about summer vacations?
What is the most difficult job you've had?
What is the most important promotion you've received?
What have been your most memorable wedding anniversaries?
What family traditions have we always followed?
What national events have most affected your life?
What was the greatest disappointment you experienced?

Stones

After weeks of labor, the children completed their stone carvings. Their teacher Joan invited them to take another class with her in the summer, but it didn't work for our schedule. Or maybe the truth is that the children were not as enthusiastic about carving as I was on their behalf. Maybe I wanted them to carve stone in order to know their grandmother. Maybe I wanted their sculptures to place in our glass-fronted cabinet amid the china, so that I could pause there and look upon the shapes they willed onto stone, so I could try to read the stories they inscribed there.

Mothers & Words

"In the past, the virtue of women's writing often lay in its divine spontaneity, like that of the blackbird's song or the thrush's. It was untaught; it was from the heart. But it was also, and much more often, chattering and garrulous—mere talk spilt over paper and left to dry in pools and blots," Woolf writes dismissively in "Women and Fiction." Her description makes me think of Martha's writing—impetuous, chatty, aloof, obscuring more than revealing. Her story is often a string of vapid anecdotes about a privileged life, with little connective tissue. Perhaps it's that the questions don't get at her story, don't give her the freedom to rove, or don't probe deeply enough. They don't elicit all she could tell. The writing prompts are the wrong ones. But she also resists many of them, leaving questions unanswered, pages of unfilled lines.

I feel disconnected from her life as a Los Angeles debutante, her life as a college student at Wellesley in the 1950s. When she claims a chasm between herself with her West Coast upbringing and the young Northeastern women she encountered in college, I don't have the context to understand. She was immensely privileged and so were her classmates. I see both worlds as exceedingly distant, virtually interchangeable, but for minor geographic variations. I see her full embrace of the marriage plot, and later, what seems to be her complete rejection of it (despite the fact that she legally still had a husband somewhere on a ranch in Washington), but her emotional transformation is absent from the pages she filled. And so, her image in my mind shimmers, refusing to coalesce into a person, her stories full of gaps and elisions, her true self remaining a mystery to me. I cannot conjure her out of the words she left behind.

A debutante and a foreign service wife, she was highly skilled at working a room, at making small talk—to the point that it seemed to become her primary mode of communication. Her children have this gift as well; Doug can chatter about nothing in particular with virtually anyone for hours. I, on the other hand, find small talk difficult and enervating; I am a person who doesn't speak unless I have something to say. And perhaps this is the difference between us: that for me, words reveal, while for Martha, words serve to obscure, to keep people at arm's length, to erect the boundaries that were necessary for her to maintain the self she had constructed. She is "chattering and garrulous," or she writes with "mindless cheer," or her words are mere "female chatter" because they serve to protect her, to keep her whole, to hold at bay anyone who would place demands on her. *I've completed my responsibilities to everyone.* Nestled there in her chatter are occasional searing lines, both revelatory and enigmatic, that keep coming back to me.

Stones & Words

Charlotte Perkins Gilman, diagnosed with terminal cancer, "preferred chloroform to cancer," ending her life at the age of seventy-five in 1935 in Pasadena, California (two months after Martha was born, just a few miles away). She considered euthanasia "the simplest of human rights," viewing her death as her final work of activism. She was an active agent of her own dying, just as she was of her own living.

Woolf famously filled her pockets with stones and walked into the River Ouse to end her life at the age of fifty-nine in 1941. Suffering another mental health crisis, she had left a note for her husband, Leonard Woolf, writing, "I feel certain that I am going mad again. I feel we can't go through another of those terrible times. And I shan't recover this time. I begin to hear voices, and I can't concentrate. So I am doing what seems the best thing to do."

Heilbrun once wrote that she would end her life on her seventieth birthday. She waited until she was seventy-seven. "She wanted to control her destiny," her son Robert said, after her suicide in 2003. "The journey is over," she wrote. "Love to all."

Martha sometimes spoke of suicide to her adult children. She would tell them, in a matter-of-fact manner, that she would be ending her life at sixty. And then it became sixty-five. It was a moving target, but the underlying rationale was clear: She would never relinquish her independence. She would control her life to the end.

Her death came swiftly. She went to the hospital one day with abdominal pain and was dead by the next morning. She was seventy-seven. Her eldest son, a doctor, flew to Mexico to handle arrangements. There was no funeral service.

Doug planted a blue hydrangea in our yard in her memory. It flourished for the seven years we continued to live in that house, and then we moved away.

Words

I never completed my red-winged blackbird project. I became a master naturalist school dropout. Still, even after the Saturday classes ended, I continued to tag along on the occasional field trips the group organized. One chilly November day, I found myself walking in the woods with ecologist Tom Wessels, an expert on New England landscapes. We were looking at stone fences.

"I call the stone fences of New England the eighth wonder of the world," Wessels told our group. "I estimate there are 250,000 miles of stone fences in New England, most of them built within a thirty-year period between 1810 and 1840. In mass, they are greater than the Great Pyramids of Egypt."

Suddenly, I could see the ghosts of people moving over the earth, lugging stones, making their mark on the land, inscribing it with their ownership. Wessels, with his Walt Whitman beard wagging, divined what had happened here. The others looked at him in awe, but as I gazed over the crumbling walls meandering through forest, I felt only despair. By 1900, Wessels explained, more than half of the cleared lands in New England had been abandoned. We paused to peer at the size of rocks in a section of fence; Wessels talked of crop fields, hay fields, pastures, logging activities. He pointed out pillows and cradles in the forest floor. All of these were clues, part of forest forensics, that allowed us to reconstruct the history of human manipulation of the land. He read stories in the rubble, but the only plot I saw was the one of our inevitable annihilation. I imagined Martha's carefully sculpted stones reduced to rubble, the futility of our endeavors against the tide of time. She forsook human relationships to shape stones, and she wrote the ending of her own story, dying surrounded by her art, beholden to no one. I understood that I would never make such an absolute and selfish choice, picking myself over others, my art over people. I saw that I would live my life in the shadows of ambivalence, as most of us do.

When I arrived home that evening, I took my children's sculptures out of the glass-fronted cabinet and felt their heft in my hands—my son's a roan-colored cliff, my daughter's a crystal-white glacier—and relished their weight, so contrary to my natural medium of words, which are made of air, even less than air. But stones did not speak to me as words did; more importantly, they did not speak *for* me. They were not enough, and they would never be enough. I would always choose words, as imprecise and inadequate as they are. I had been searching all my life for a language that would express my experiences with purity, with precision, but I always came up against the limits of language. Perhaps this was what appealed most to me about birds: They say exactly what they mean. Birdsong is a pure clarion call of existence. And in my naming of things, in my quest for accuracy and sharpness, perhaps I was striving for that same clarity. This was the whole point in my naming of the natural world—*Agelaius phoeniceus, Quercus alba, Ardea herodias*—for in noticing and speaking what was around me, I anchored myself to the physical world, the tenuous, abstract tethers of language securing me to the corporeal. In naming, I took the rasp of meaning to my life and hewed out of it something sharp-edged and recognizable, wrenching from the murky sea of time an utterance all my own, finally crafting a sentence that said something of who I am, making the meaning of my life briefly blaze forth like the red torches of sumac in a riotous forest landscape.

Interlude BIRDS I'VE KNOWN

I remember the birds in the painting my mother made me stare at and analyze. It was a reproduction, a scene of spindly trees and snow and birds. *Grachi,* they're called in Russian.

Then there were the pet parakeets I got when I was eight. The first one, green and yellow, I named Ptichka—Russian for little bird. It made me believe the bird was Russian—or partially so—just as my Russian first name made me at least nominally Russian. So when the birdcage fell from its hook in the ceiling in the living room and smashed open on the floor during one of our earthquakes, it seemed fitting that Ptichka flew up to the top of a tall bookcase in the corner filled with the Russian classics my mother had hauled with her to California when she and I left Russia five years before. Ptichka just perched there, sitting atop Tolstoy and Dostoevsky, waiting for rescue. Or for whatever came next.

I could not glean much from the painting, which, my mother told me in Russian, depicts the return of the grachi. My mother asked me pointed questions—What time of year is it? Winter, I guessed. No, grachi would not be returning in winter. But there is snow on the ground, I weakly objected. That is not fresh snow, my mother scolded. That is melting snow. I shrugged. I knew snow only from books. Russia might as well be Mars. We had no great spring thaw. Our Mediterranean climate meant seasons were nearly indistinguishable, one casually shrugging into the next—windbreaker on, windbreaker off. Some people—like one of my uncles—wore shorts year-round. There were always birds around, as far as I could tell. They came and went whenever they felt like it, perching on palm trees and orange trees and jacarandas.

In what I considered my greatest childhood work of art—the one picture I felt captured my soaring vision as an artist—a periwinkle bird sits high on a branch overlooking a vast landscape dotted with the even dark nubs of orange trees, stretching as far as the eye can see, with purple mountains rising in the distance.

My second parakeet, which was blue, I named Blue. In English. In Russian, there are two words for blue—*goluboy* and *siniy*, light blue and dark blue. There is no single Russian word that encompasses all of English *blue*. Wanting my bird to have options, I gave it the English word.

My mother has always called herself *sova*—an owl—because she stays up all night. She doesn't sleep. That's how she knows so much: She reads thousands of books while the weak sleep.

Once, my American uncles rescued an injured crow and put it in a cage in the yard. I sat right next to it for the week or two of its rehabilitation, stared into its coal black glint of an eye. What did it know? What did it think of me? There's a photo somewhere of me with that bird.

In Russia, my aunt kept birds too—canaries who sang. Until the cat ate them. Or they flew out the *fortochka*. Or both. I will need to corroborate these stories. My aunt is dead now, but my mother will remember.

I no longer tolerate pet birds—their squawking and pooping, the halo of seed shells around their cages.

Wild birds are another matter. In Denali I watched golden eagles for hours on end. And don't get me started on loons.

I once tried to study red-winged blackbirds in a wetland near my house in Connecticut, but the only stories I could tell about them were really stories about me.

I've never known a bird for itself. Only for how I want it to be.

Grachi, I later learned, are rooks. But I'm not really sure what rooks are.

In English the painting is known as *The Rooks Have Returned.* It was painted in 1871 by Russian artist Alexei Savrasov. Looking at it now, forty years later, I remember my mother's disappointment in my inability to have thoughts about paintings and to express those thoughts in Russian. My Russian sometimes came out as guttural caws, while my English could be as intricate as the most complex vocalization of a songbird. But it must mean something that I am able, now, to describe the painting well enough to find it online. Wikipedia identifies the painting as the "high point" of Savrasov's artistic career and gives the kind of analysis my mother probably wanted me to give (but in Russian): "Using a common, even trivial, episode of birds returning home, and an extremely simple landscape, Savrasov emotionally showed the transition of nature from winter to spring." He painted in the *lyrical landscape* style, also called the *mood landscape,* which sounds exactly like what I'm trying to do much of the time, except in words.

I recently started reading a book about the evolution of birds. I learned that *Archaeopteryx,* one of the earliest genera, is both bird and dinosaur. And dinosaurs may have had feathers. The categories of the world grow ever more unstable. I plan to finish that book someday, but I'm taking a break.

My American grandfather had a parrot that sat on his shoulder, his constant companion. He loved that bird more than he did most people. Or at least he loved it with a less complicated kind of love. For a while, he got its wings clipped, but then the bird seemed to forget that it could fly, so he didn't bother to keep clipping its wings. You know how this story ends. One day, when they were out in the yard, the bird took flight, and he never saw it again.

Birds are like that.

Isle Royale National Park

ISLAND LIFE, WITH BOY

Postcard Dispatches from
Isle Royale National Park, Michigan
July 2021

Embarking

As you travel down the Keweenaw Waterway toward Lake Superior aboard the *Ranger III*, you watch houses and trees through the window, a moving postcard. A runner loping along a trail following the waterway appears in view, running inside your postcard, and as you watch him, you think how miraculous it is that you're both alive on this one day, that he and you have both ended up here, that he has become part of your life, even if he doesn't know of your existence. But what, really, do you know of his? That he is young and strong, that he runs on this beautiful sunny morning along a waterway in the Upper Peninsula, that he seems to love being alive—or so his stride tells you. You tell your boy, who is sitting beside you, about the runner, but he is engrossed in maps. Finally, out on the lake, your postcard flatlines, registering just water and horizon line. You are going to a place you have never been, where you will see sights you've never seen. A ranger's voice erupts from the PA system, telling you about the place you're going, "a mystical land full of moose and wolves."

Mental Maps

If Lake Superior is a wolf's head, then Isle Royale is the eye, peering west over northernmost Minnesota. And if Isle Royale is the eye, then Dassler Point is near the lateral canthus. But up close, Isle Royale doesn't look like an eye. A 1914 travel brochure describes the main island as "fringed with hundreds of small and scenic islands, like diamonds encircling a brilliant emerald or sapphire, each a natural gem in the silvered sea, rock-anchored and foliage-wreathed." Your sketches of your location look like the head of an open-ended spanner wrench, your cabin at Dassler on one point, Scoville on the other point, with your rocky beach in the opening between the jaws. For a century, people have lived on this point among rocks and trees and sky—first, the Dasslers of Leavenworth, Kansas, summer after summer, camping and then building structures. For the past three decades, the cabin has housed artists-in-residence. On the first day, your boy is turned around and can't find the outhouse or the boathouse, but with each day, you explore and add detail to your mental maps. Soon, he is bounding up and down the crisscrossing trails. Soon, you know this place by heart.

Space Pioneer

"What is that orange on the rocks?" you ask your motorboat captain on your first ride to your cabin. "Lichen," he tells you, and you realize you've never paid heed to lichen before—not really, not in the way it deserves. It's as though an artist dabbed final touches on the landscape, the perfect accent. And yet it is no afterthought. "Pioneering lichens probably preceded all other life to Isle Royale's bare, glacier-scoured rocks thousands of years ago," a sign on the trail informs you. On Dassler beach you begin a lichen study, poring over a minuscule ginger sunburst, noting the astonishing complexity of this algae and fungi union. You once met a poet in Denali who sought poems in whatever would fit in an eight-inch square—a patch of tundra, a wolf print. You could write an entire tome on a solitary square inch. One evening, in town, you spot a book on lichens through the window of the closed visitor center. You come back for it later, and you learn that elegant sunburst lichen, *Xanthoria elegans*, was sent to space to test its ability to survive an interplanetary journey. After 14.6 days, it returned unscathed, fully able to photosynthesize.

Ambitions, Aspirations

At first you wonder—how will you fill your days? What will you do? But then, rather than suppressing the stimuli of your surroundings—the modus operandi of your non-island life—you burgeon with just being here. The island engorges you. You spend an hour drawing the screen door, its fish-shaped iron handle. This is how animals live, in a constant now. "I think I could turn and live with animals," Walt Whitman whispers in your head, "they are so placid and self-contain'd." The ceaseless pricking anxieties of non-island life transform into mild ambitions, aspirations, smooth as sea-worn stones. Draw wood lilies. Play Scrabble. Skip a rock more than three skips. Find northern paintbrush. Pay attention to trees. Find out why air currents on Scoville sometimes bring a sudden puff of heat. Float in the canoe on a still evening and take pictures. Draw maps. Read about loons. Write a postcard to your husband and other child back home living their non-island lives. Row the laundry to town. Think about wolves. Draw the fireplace. Read poem scraps in mouse-nibbled envelope. The boy has his own ambition, bigger than yours: to see the other end of the island, to circumnavigate it.

Scoville Point, Night

The Junior Ranger booklet instructs the boy to spend ten minutes outside in the dark, but a week in, he still hasn't managed. At the apex of summer, twilight lingers past bedtime. One night, going to the outhouse, you're so startled by stars you change course, stumbling out onto the craggy rocks. You sit under the hush of a jeweled sky and form a new ambition: to bring the boy here, to gaze at the fiercely burning stars, to think of the dark island and all the life that teems here, all the hearts, large and small, slow and fast, adamantly beating out life's tempo. A line from an essay by Brian Doyle flits through your mind: "Every creature on earth has approximately two billion heartbeats to spend in a lifetime." Some burn them up in a year, and some ration them over a hundred years. You think about the hearts that are winking out tonight all over the island in ceaseless waves of death and the ones flashing on for the first time, and you see those hearts in your mind like fireflies, like stars.

Alces alces

You encounter your first island moose on the Fourth of July, when you and the boy are down on your dock, drawing in your notebooks, watching the light fade over Tobin Harbor. You are about to head back when you hear a thrashing, a pummeling and tearing of foliage, directly behind the boathouse. Then you hear the distinct sound of masticating. You won't be going anywhere just yet. You draw a new picture of your boathouse, your green canoe tucked in behind, which is really a picture of a moose feeding at dusk, of the unseen. Sometimes the things you cannot see loom larger than the things you can. When the moose moves away, when you hear nothing for five minutes, ten, you finally creep—your boy leading the way—toward your cabin. You are nearly there, rounding the bend in the trail, when you come upon the moose, whom the boy later names Matilda, standing directly in front of your door. She looks at you, and you look back. You will not be going home just yet. You retreat down to your beach, where you wait in the gloaming.

Just Tilted Rocks

One of the signs you pass daily on the Stoll Trail is titled "Isle Royale: just tilted rocks." It explains: "All of Isle Royale is a series of ridges and valleys formed by huge tilted layers of rock." In the cabin, you pore over the work of previous artists-in-residence collected in a book, *The Island Within Us*. Ladislav Hanka, artist-in-residence in 1992, writes, "For me the dominant feeling of Isle Royale and consequently of the artwork I produced there is of geology stripped bare—life being but the thinnest of membranes stretched precariously taut, clinging to nearly barren rock." One day, you spy a fallen tree near the trail. It has come untethered from the ground, the tentacled mass of its root ball on display—except rather than being a ball, the roots form a pancake, spreading ten feet or more across but no more than six inches deep. The tree had been growing in just a few inches of soil, clinging tenaciously to rock. You examine the miracle of the root-pancake from every angle, while your boy impatiently urges you on. "Are you done yet?" he wants to know. "But look at this pancake!" you keep exclaiming.

Island Palette

You have a new craving for all things orange; you study them, draw them, drink them in. You covet not just the lichen but also the wood lily, the honey-drenched sliver of a moon tinted orange by smoke from distant fires. You wear down your *yellowed orange* colored pencil again and again, along with *Spanish orange, sunburst yellow, goldenrod, yellow ochre, sand, pale vermilion.* You sharpen the oranges, the blues, the grays. Lake Superior eats up *peacock blue, jade green, light cerulean blue, cloud blue,* except the days it's brooding. Then the water and the rocks devour so much gray: *warm, cool,* and *French gray, putty beige, ginger root.* You study Lake Superior to learn its moods and hues. Sometimes, the water is olive green, sometimes pure white, nearly merging with sky. Sometimes the water transforms from silver to inky to moss to slate to rose to wine in a single day. If you were a painter, you would create a long, narrow canvas to show the stretch of this place, how life unfurls horizontally. You made a mistake when you brought your regular sketchbook with its portrait orientation. The island demands landscape layout, room to unspool.

Scoville Point, Night

Your new ambition burns in you: to take the boy out to see stars. But a haze has descended, and night after night, when you drag yourself outside, there are barely any stars, just a few dim pinpricks. Regret swarms you. Why didn't you take him out the night stars were spilled across the sky? You orchestrate the adventure in your mind: scrambling over rocks, the soothing stroke of waves, the brimming sky. "What do you want most in the world?" you will ask him. What will he say? Is he even glad he came on this trip? Would he prefer to be working on his online coding class in the comfort of central AC, a flush toilet down the hall? Your question is perhaps too big. You would have had no answer at thirteen—not one that meant anything. What do *you* want most in the world? You turn the question on yourself. To come to more places like this, to have more nights like this, to not squander the heartbeats you have left. As always, you are writing your life before it happens. Later, you'll be disappointed when it doesn't follow the script. And even when it does.

Outreach

You had planned to offer visitors small pieces of cardstock, pens, colored pencils, and then to create postcards with them about their experiences in the park. Ranger Tina taught you this in Denali six years ago. *Dear non-island self,* you imagined visitors writing. *Today I heard the prehistoric rattle of a sandhill crane, the warning slap of beaver tail on water, the song of the surf on stone. Please never forget this.* You imagined them drawing a swimming moose, a sunny ridge thrumming with dragonflies, lichen-encrusted crags. But the ongoing pandemic has shut down all public programming. There is no outreach, so you reach out to yourself, writing these postcards to your non-island self. You think of Barry Lopez's idea of two landscapes—the one within and the one without—and the ways "the interior landscape responds to the character and subtlety of an exterior landscape." You pay attention to both, doing what writers-in-residence have done for decades. In 1991 artist-in-residence Keith Taylor wrote about "the extraordinary opportunity of watching myself learn to see a new landscape." Thirty years later, you continue his work. Dear non-island self, remember this always.

Voyageurs

You hike all the trails near your cabin, to Lookout Louise, Mount Franklin, Lane Cove, Three Mile Campground, Siskowit Mine. You do several fifteen-mile days, venturing farther and farther from home. Still, the boy wants to see more. You book tickets on the *Voyageur II* to go look at the other end of the island. You borrow a tent from Ranger Katie to camp at Washington Creek. You're told that most artists-in-residence never go to Windigo; every five years or so one will make the trek. On the boat ride, you take in the island's span with your eyes. It feels important, to see it from all sides, to take its full measure. "Have you reckon'd the earth much?" Walt Whitman asks. You are reckoning the island, this eye in the wolf's head that is the world's largest freshwater lake by surface area. You hike ten miles to see Huginnin Cove and Windigo Mine. The forest is more spacious here, the trees bigger, with less rock laid bare. Your boy declares he likes your end of the island better, but still, this isn't bad. "Are you looking at lichen again?" he yells, when you fall behind. You're always falling behind.

Canoe Float

The canoe float is a genre of adventure the boy doesn't understand. What is the point of aimless drifting? He wants a destination, so you invent goals: Row to Smith Island, land on the small spit of land on the west side. Pretend you are explorers, the first ones to ever set foot here. Try to penetrate the vegetation. Discover the island is full of bees. Hunker down on the tiny beach, look for beautiful rocks and sea glass. Get back in the canoe, circumnavigate Smith. Gaze up at your beloved bench on Dassler Point, the place you've spent so many hours with your notebook. Paddle up Tobin Harbor, get a closer look at the pieces of the collapsed fish house that have been lovingly laid out on the shore, awaiting possible reconstruction. Float slowly back to your dock, pushed by a gentle breeze, resisting the urge to paddle. Floating is the point of a canoe float, you have to tell your impatient boy. When you get back to the cabin, place your gorgeous piece of sea glass from Smith Island on the mantel with the others collected there over the years.

Questions While Hiking

Are beavers brilliant? How many days are in six months? Are there more cups in the world than people? If you weren't here, where would you want to be? Why do flowers waste so much energy making large, colorful petals? Is there a liquid less viscous than water? Would it make enormous splashes if you threw rocks into it? Could you float in it? How many people are on the island right now? How many otters? If flotsam floats and jetsam washes up, what do you call something that sinks to the bottom? If you could have any superpower, what would you choose? Why does the sun look like a dim red disk? How many time zones are there? How did the moose get here? What is a portico? Why did the *Edmund Fitzgerald* sink? What do wolves think about? What do their mental maps look like? Do they know the contour of every ridge, every shoreline? Do animals know where they are? Do they look out across the water and imagine a life somewhere else? Do they think of other places? What does it mean to know where you are? What do you want most in the world?

Scoville Point, Night

The sky finally clears, and you take the boy out on the rocks, and the stars burn fiercely, but none of the rest of it happens according to script. The boy is so tired he can hardly keep his eyes open. He answers your questions with grunts, finally says, "I'm tired," so you go back. But you did it, right? You saw the messiness of the Milky Way, like the effusive paint spatters left behind from a majestic masterpiece you cannot see, your senses able to apprehend only what's left on the studio floor. You recognize only the sloppiness of creation: spattered stars, tilted rocks, riots of vegetation. You think: What you wanted can't be manufactured, planned. You don't know this yet, but two evenings later, you and the boy will glide in your canoe on water still and clear as a windowpane and hear loons speak their antediluvian language, and the moment will unexpectedly arrest you: the loons blazing as brightly as stars on the water. And this will be so much more than the exhausted scrabble over rocks in the night.

Simplicity

A nibbled, yellowing envelope, stored inside a Ziploc bag, contains "beginnings of poems" that artist-in-residence Gary Lawless left in June of 1997, along with other scraps, written in many hands, from a community poem activity organized in August 2001. *Gray-green lichen has created a ghost tree. The cry of the loons echoes my sadness.* One contains a single word: *Simplicity*. Yes, simplicity is apt: You have been simply eating, sleeping, reading, hiking, canoeing, looking at the sky, sweeping the floor, washing the dishes, carrying buckets of water. Your inert black brick of a phone has slipped to the bottom of your backpack. You've had no email, texts, social media, or news for seventeen days. You have no idea what's happening in the world—except for the fires in Canada that have smoked over your sky, except what your senses have told you. *What do you want most in the world?* You write your question on a scrap, add it to the envelope. On board the *Ranger III* on the ride back to Houghton, as passengers abandon puzzles and games to stare at their phones in silence, you write: *I cannot believe I have to go back.*

Reprinted with permission from the National Park Service.
A longer version of this essay with photographs can be found on the NPS website at https://www.nps.gov/isro/getinvolved/air-renfro-island-life-with-boy.htm.

Isle Royale National Park

LOON BOY

Isle Royale National Park, Michigan
July 2021

-1-

We were rowing back across Tobin Harbor when we saw the loons.

By then, we had been two weeks on Isle Royale, the island national park in Lake Superior, and we had canoed in the harbor and seen loons at least half a dozen times. This was not even a pleasure row, but more of a commute. It was nearing dusk, and we were returning from our most strenuous day of hiking yet—a sixteen-mile trek—and we still had to row a mile across the harbor to reach our cabin.

Our day already burgeoned with sights—the moose we startled on the trail that snorted and pounded the ground in hasty retreat, the sandhill cranes that croaked their prehistoric cry over the slate blue waters of Lake Superior before taking flight—and I was grateful that the water was now placid, that we could easily weave our way among the small islands that dotted the harbor. I was done with the day, ready to boil the kettle on the camp stove for ramen, then strap on a headlamp and read aloud from a worn 1944 paperback of *Famous Ghost Stories* with my thirteen-year-old son, who was my companion on this adventure. My thoughts were on putting the day away for good, tucking it into the past.

And it was then, when we rounded Glenns Island, that we suddenly came upon the loons: an adult in its striking and intricate black and white nuptial plumage being closely trailed by a fuzzy brownish-gray juvenile. Perhaps fifteen feet from our canoe, they seemed unconcerned about our presence. We immediately stopped rowing.

The adult looked out across the water, away from us, and then it vocalized, calling out its long, haunting wail, as though crying its own name. *Looooooooon.* In the distance, we saw a speck on the water, another loon approaching. *Looooooooon,* it responded in the same plaintive register. The three loons—the two adults and the juvenile—joined up and floated together on the still surface of the water. And we kept watching.

When we arrived on the island, the babies had been so small that they rode on their parents' backs—from a distance, we sometimes spotted the downy tufts adorning the black-speckled backs of adults. We had always steered clear of the loons—as instructed by park rangers. But these loons didn't seem to notice us. One of the rangers had told us that because the park was barely operational last year due to the pandemic—the commercial boats didn't run all season—there were more loons than ever in Tobin Harbor. Even though people had returned this year, the loons seemed unfazed. Perhaps two people in a canoe were barely worth their notice. With motorized boats on the water and the seaplanes roaring in multiple times a day overhead—their summer home becoming a runway, or the runway being their home—maybe the loons were inured to us, the quiet, unmotorized version of human. Still, we didn't want to start rowing again, startling them, breaking the stillness.

And then suddenly, without perceptible communication, both of the adults dove underwater, and the scrappy little chick was left floating by itself on the surface. We watched it bobbing there in the adults' wake. My son spoke quietly.

"Do you think it wonders where its parents went?"

- 2 -

On April 12, 1961, Soviet cosmonaut Yuri Gagarin became the first man to orbit the earth when he was flung into space inside a metal sphere. His single orbit lasted 108 minutes. This happened before I was born—as indeed had all of the 1960s space race—yet people still argued over who had won. The Russians had the first man in space. OK, granted, but the Americans put the first man on the moon. I had heard these arguments countless times in my childhood, but to me, it didn't matter. With a Russian mother and American father, with a Soviet passport and an American address, I got to win the space race either way.

I pictured him plunging into space, that miraculous dive into the unknown. The son of a carpenter, of peasant stock, he actually rode a rocket ship into space—the stuff of science fiction. With a name that was easy to pronounce and transliterate, with his broad boyish grin, he was a ready-made hero of the people. How could you not love him—with his affable nature, that smile that could melt hearts all over the world. He smiled more than any Russian I have ever known. "I have never seen such a smile anywhere," remarked the daughter of Pavel Popovich, one of Gagarin's fellow cosmonauts. "Direct, like the sun. Like a light bulb. Everything around it lit up."

Even his backup—the man he was selected over—the intellectual, Pushkin-quoting Gherman Titov, recognized his lovable nature. "I'm not lovable," Titov said in one of the last interviews before his death. "I'm telling you, they were right to choose Yura." Though he would be the second cosmonaut in space, though he would orbit the earth seventeen times and be the first human being to spend over a day in space, how many people, aside from historians and space race aficionados, know Titov's name now? He understood that Gagarin, the lovable boy-cosmonaut, would always outshine him. Gagarin was picked because he was so wonderfully himself. We had to love the man we were lobbing into orbit. This was important, in case he survived, actually returned alive. In case we had to revere him forever as a hero. By some accounts, his chance at succeeding was just 46 percent. Meanwhile, NASA kept Alan Shepard on the ground because the chance of his success was calculated at only 98 percent. That was one reason the Russians got a man up first: a greater tolerance for risk.

The spring Gagarin made his flight, my mother was fifteen years old, living in Kuybyshev, an industrial city on the Volga River. The ice was just breaking up on the river during the spring thaw. That day, she was rehearsing with her school choir when the news came: A Soviet cosmonaut had gone into space. The students were dismissed, given the rest of the day off in celebration. Instead of going home, my mother and her friend Lyuda made their way to the Volga, where they watched the ice floes. Suddenly, the ice they were standing on broke away, and they began to be swept out into the frigid river. At that moment, out of nowhere, their classmate Volodya Migunov appeared and rescued them, somehow wrenching them back onto the beach. My mother doesn't know how he managed to save the both of them, but he did—and then he vanished. They were not lost to the icy torrents after all. Gagarin had gone into space, and they were still alive.

My father, eighteen years old, was finishing his first year of college in his native Southern California. The flight left little lasting impression on him. He had yet to discover his deep passion for Slavic languages, which would eventually lead him to graduate school, to Russia, to my mother. On that April day, they were still over a dozen years from knowing one another.

It seemed apropos of nothing that I had started thinking about Gagarin while serving as artist-in-residence on a remote island park in Lake Superior, sixty years and three months after his flight. But nothing is ever apropos of nothing. Wasn't it odd, I thought, how I had started thinking of him here, of all places? Wasn't it strange how the mind works? I tried to figure out a connection but could find none. Perhaps it was just that I'd been looking at the nighttime sky, blazing with more stars than I'd seen in years. But this felt inaccurate, or at least incomplete. And I was cut off from the internet, with no phone service, no Google. Not that Google would be able to offer a satisfying answer to my pressing question: Google, why am I thinking about Yuri Gagarin on Isle Royale? There are many things Google doesn't know.

-3-

As we drifted in the canoe, I thought about the book I was reading in our cabin: *Call of the Loon* by Paul Strong. The loons' wail, which he describes as "a long, drawn-out call that sounds like the howl of a wolf," is used to bring two loons that are far apart closer together. A mated pair often speaks to one another this way, as we had just witnessed. Unlike most birds, loons have solid bones, making them heavy enough to dive two hundred feet, but their weight makes take-off a challenge. Strong describes the loon as a "feathered fish" that is "sometimes more finny than feathery," living on the "razor's edge" between life in the water and life in the sky.

Worried that our presence was what prompted the loons to dive, my son suggested that we gently row away from the chick, to give it space. A short distance out, we stopped and drifted, watching, waiting for the loons to surface. The chick bobbed on our small waves.

"What if they don't come back?" my son asked.

"Do you remember the first time you went hiking?" I said, and then I told him the story. He was just two, and we were visiting my parents in Southern California, in the neighborhood where I grew up. Trailheads to the Box Springs Mountains are accessible a half a mile from my parents' house in a 1950s subdivision. On a foggy day, my brother and I took him on an easy trail on a low hill. At first, we all walked together, but I grew impatient at the pace and went ahead, disappearing into the fog. Suddenly my son started calling for me with such despair that I understood he thought we were separated forever. His uncle picked him up to carry him, but he was inconsolable. "Mooooom! Moooooooom!" he wailed mournfully, though I was just twenty feet away. Of course, I circled back and returned to him.

As I came to the end of my story, the loons still had not surfaced. And then another loon, far up the harbor, sounded its tremolo, that maniacal laugh that is as famous as the wail. One of my guidebooks suggested that I would hear the "eerie, demented laugh" so incessantly that I would imagine the voice of a lunatic perpetually cackling just outside my cabin window. But the actual tremolos we had heard were distant and far between, the vocalization subtler, more expressive. Strong writes that the tremolo is a call of alarm, given when a loon is disturbed or threatened. By now, I had heard the call a number of times, echoing through the harbor.

But this time, I heard something new in the tremolo. The loon seemed to be speaking a word I could almost, just barely, understand. I felt a glimmer—an awakening of something I had once known. I knew I knew something, but I didn't know what it was.

-4-

Many Russian last names are formed from common nouns. For example, Yablokov comes from *yabloko,* apple; Lebedev from *lebed',* swan; Komarov from *komar,* mosquito; Kamenev from *kamen',* stone; Morozov from *moroz*, frost. My mother's maiden name, Stulova, comes from the word *stul*, or chair. In almost all cases, I knew the name of the common noun before I ever encountered the surname. So when I see Lebedev, I think swan-man, and Yablokov is apple-man, and Medvedev, bear-man.

Occasionally, though, I learned a surname before I ever learned the noun from which it is derived, and nowhere is that truer than in the name Gagarin. I had known his name for as long as I can remember. It meant cosmonaut, space-man. It meant national hero, space race triumph. It meant Soviet might. By the time I got here, Gagarin was already reduced—transformed—into a series of statues and hard-lined steel monuments soaring upward, images on postage stamps and coins. By the time I got here, his heroism, his sanctity, was galvanized by his being dead. His thirty-four years of life had blazed and burned out. He had been lost, finally, to aviation—not in space, but in a routine training flight on a more ordinary aircraft. He left behind a wife and two young daughters. One day, their father dove back into the sky and didn't successfully resurface. One day there was no safe return.

-5-

There is a category of word that lives in my mind in two separate rooms, the English room and the Russian room, and the door between them has remained shut. Common objects—a spoon, for example—always lived in my head in both languages simultaneously, the door between thrown wide open. Spoon and lozhka. I knew all the common animals, domestic and barnyard: dog and sobaka, cow and korova. I knew the exotic zoo animals: elephant and slon, rhinoceros and nosorog. But that category of flora and fauna that lived out in the world, distant from me, that was neither domestic nor exotic, that was part of the landscape, part of the wild—the trees and plants, the fish and birds—is where the partition was, where the words didn't connect.

Part of this was the effect of geography—two radically different places, one Old World and one New, would not be home to all the same flora and fauna. But perhaps more than this, these were species that could be encountered by spending time in the outdoors or pursuing field guides or natural history books, which were not the kind of books my parents read or collected. Of course, I amassed a great many tree names: maple, oak, poplar, pine, fir, and so on. And the same was true in Russian: dub, klyon, yel', lipa. But most of these lived in their separate rooms. Only as an adult, only with intentional effort, did I open some of the doors: klyon is maple, yel' is spruce. I taught myself that grachi are rooks, that lastochki are swallows.

Another part of the problem is lack of exposure. Prior to coming to Isle Royale, I had never to my knowledge seen a living loon to which my concept of loon could adhere. A loon, until then, was just a ghostly avian abstraction. I did not hail from northern lake country. And yet I had known of loons, perhaps due to their "cult status," as Strong describes it, that began in the 1970s, when "the loon gained status as a symbol of wild, unspoiled things." Loons appear on shirts, bumper stickers, wall art, furniture, and jewelry. And their vocalizations are popular Hollywood sound effects, appearing in countless films and TV shows. The 1981 film *On Golden Pond,* which I had watched as a child, prominently features loons and their distinctive calls. "Whenever a producer wants to say you're far from civilization (or help), in goes the wail," writes Minnesota writer Frank Bures.

Though I had come to associate the English word *loon* with its wail—the long, haunting cry of a bird speaking its own name—the word is not in fact onomatopoeic. Rather, it derives from a Scandinavian word meaning clumsy, for the way the bird lumbers on land. Its association with insanity, according to Hartford Courant language columnist Rob Kyff, is coincidental: "What's fascinating is that the 'loon' meaning a mentally unbalanced person, while originally derived from the Middle English 'loun,' has been seriously amped up in its 'crazy' meaning by two other linguistic power sources: 'lunatic' (an insane person) and 'loon' (a slightly unhinged bird)."

In Britain the bird is called the great northern diver, and the French word also refers to the bird's diving ability. Indigenous peoples in North America called the birds too-lik, hakweem, kwee-moo, and mahng (which means "brave-hearted one"). In every language, the word for loon refers to only one facet of who they are. And not all loons are the same. There are five living species of loon within the genus *Gavia*; the common loon of North America is distinct from Eurasian species. I am not intending to conflate all loons. And yet, perhaps I am.

Because here is the incredible claim I have been building toward: that evening when we were sitting in the canoe and I heard that loon cackling out its tremolo far up the harbor, it spoke to me in Russian. These two birds—the one who wailed its doleful looooooon over the water, and the one now sounding out its ululating laugh—suddenly coalesced and became one in my mind. I remembered a faint echo of a fact I once knew: that *gagara* is a noun that means diving bird. Suddenly, a door flew open, the fresh-faced smiling cosmonaut transforming into a diving bird, a loon boy. In that moment, I understood that *gagara* must mean loon, or *loon* must mean gagara—they had the same referent. Through some backdoor of my mind, my thoughts led me here: I had been thinking about Gagarin since my arrival on the island because the first time I heard a loon's tremolo, I heard it speaking its Russian name. Gagara.

-6-

A five-year-old girl was planting potatoes in a field with her grandmother when she saw something orange and beautiful descending from the sky. Her grandmother grew frightened and grabbed the girl's hand, intending to rush back to the house, but by then the apparition was coming across the field and speaking. The girl said, "Grandma, stop. Listen. He's speaking Russian. He's probably human."

It's a fairy tale ending: a man falling from the sky, making that plunge back to Earth—a kind of reverse surfacing, a return to life, to air, to breath. I imagine the girl and her dumbfounded grandmother. The logical conclusion that someone who speaks Russian must be human—or someone who is human must speak Russian—is both naive and astute. For strange things had recently fallen from the sky: capsules containing space dogs, a shot-down American spy, and even a mannequin named Ivan Ivanovich, who made two flights with a whole cabinet of curiosities packed into his chest cavity, thighs, spacesuit, and in the capsule around him: forty white mice, forty black mice, guinea pigs, reptiles, plant seeds, human blood samples, cancer cells, bacteria, fermentation samples, and a dog companion. Not that the girl or her grandmother would likely know any of this.

"Where are you from?" asked the astonished grandmother. "How did you get here?"

"On a ship," the man replied.

"There's no water near here," the grandmother said. "What ship?"

"I came from the sky," said Gagarin.

Rita Nurskanova described this scene to a BBC reporter for a story that aired in April 2021, sixty years after she became the first person to greet Gagarin back to Earth when he parachuted out of his capsule. She was that five-year-old girl, helping her grandmother in a potato field in the Saratov region, not far from where my mother would attend university in just over a year.

When asked by the reporter if she remembered anything about the space-man who suddenly appeared in front of her, Nurskanova said, "His smile, of course. His smile."

-7-

Three days after our loon encounter, we would leave Isle Royale, embarking on the six-hour boat ride aboard *Ranger III* to Houghton, Michigan. A couple of hours into the trip, the other passengers, one by one, abandoned their card games and conversations, powered on their phones, and fell silent as they scrolled through the avalanche of messages awaiting them. We were back within range of cell service. I held out as long as I could—I'd been without internet for nearly three weeks, and I didn't miss it—but then I gave in, turned on my phone, and asked it my question: Are a loon and gagara indeed the same bird? They are, Google confirmed. I also learned that etymologically, the word *gagara* is onomatopoeic. A related verb, *gogotat'*, often applied to geese, means "to cackle." The loon did speak to me.

I looked over at my boy, engrossed in reading a tattered sixty-year-old mass market paperback edition of Mark Twain's complete stories that he pilfered from the cabin for the long ride back. I thought about telling him my loon news, but it could wait. One day, we will be floating in a canoe or ascending a peak or pitching a tent, and I will tell him the story of seeing the loons in Tobin Harbor when he was thirteen.

- 8 -

Of course, I can't leave those loons underwater. I have to return to Tobin Harbor, to the canoe, to our expectant wait. I have to return the chick to its parents—or the parents to their chick. It was as though we'd been holding our breath ever since the loons dove under—only of course we hadn't, since loons can stay underwater for five minutes. *What if they don't come back?* My son's question echoed in my mind. And then, twenty feet away, one of the adults broke the surface, making reentry, and the chick sailed confidently in its direction. Farther away, the second adult surfaced, and the family reunited and headed away from us into the harbor.

We started rowing toward our dock.

Some nights on the island, I had gone out after dark, after my son was asleep, and looked up at the night sky and thought about a cosmonaut in space, not yet understanding why, not yet knowing that it was a bird that had spoken his name to me. Two nights prior, I had awakened my son at two in the morning to climb out on the rocks of Scoville Point and look at the stars, the fine powder of the Milky Way, to feel small and human under a night sky, to imagine what it might be like to streak across the cosmos inside a metal ball, wondering if you will return whole, or at all. I wanted him to see the sky with me, but he was too sleepy to care, wanting only his bed. I had pictured him remembering this moment under the stars his entire life, even as an old man, decades after I was gone, but perhaps that isn't the memory that will stay with him. Perhaps it will be the loons on the still water of Tobin Harbor. Perhaps it will be that tiny pocket of time—the span it takes a loon to dive and then to resurface, to tell a story, to hear a bird speak. Who is to say what will be remembered, what will be forgotten, what doors of memory will remain closed or will be thrown open? Who is to say what is more miraculous—that initial plunge, or the safe return?

Interlude MOVING: A TRIPTYCH

1. Four Months After the Move

What can I say to cheer you up? We have lake-effect snow and there's a fence to climb and woods to explore and a neighborhood cat named Boson who comes around to rub against our ankles. You tell me none of this compares to Connecticut. One night, you and your brother stay up making a list of everything you've left behind. For example: driving down Craigmoor Road with the windows down, on your way to Big Y, while Dad rambles on about something and a breeze blows through the van. "You know this is worse for us than it is for you," you tell me, and you do the math to prove it. You've spent nearly two-thirds of your life in Connecticut, and for your brother it's over four-fifths, while I lived there only about a fifth of mine. OK, but what about the sky? Hear me out. Recently, when the sixty-year-old alumnae were on campus, I overheard two of them talking. "I miss the Indiana sky," one of them said, looking at the empty expanse over the student center, and the other echoed, "Oh, the Indiana sky!" When I looked up, the sky was cold and empty and nothing to remark on, but suddenly it seemed tinged with significance. Yes, it's dark and cold, and it will only get darker and colder before we come out the other side of winter. And yes, through this whole winter we will miss Connecticut—our life there now tinged with hindsight, the heavy nostalgia filter rendering it poignant and Instagram-ready. I have a list too. Every time I walk our old haunts in my mind—the frog pond, the red-winged blackbird thicket, the big tree—I become lost in grief for the place we left behind, the people we were. But the Indiana sky. Let's love it, even if it's the only thing we love this first winter. It's a start.

2. *Glaciation*

Sunk into the plush seats of a chartered bus, we listened to Garry the naturalist make the flat northern Indiana landscape come alive: glaciers grinding and slithering, relentless in their trudge from Canada; water brimming everywhere, today's trickle of creek once a mile wide; unimaginable drifts of sand, an entire steep neighborhood of treacherous streets erected atop a stranded dune; the Canadian rocks that sailed here on the swells and were marooned, still churning up in people's yards; the astonished well drillers who sometimes hit bedrock a dozen feet down, but other times have to drill hundreds of feet; the terminal moraines and kettle lakes that buckle and pock the land. *Picture an English muffin,* Garry told us. *That's the bedrock, with its nooks and crannies. Now picture slathering it with peanut butter, filling in those pockets, smoothing it all out. The peanut butter is what the glacier did.* In other words: Secret ancient hills slumber beneath our feet. We spent two hours on that bus with Garry, training our eyes to see a lost world. Living amid the debris of a glacier that shot its fingers down from Canada, we suddenly understood so much—for example, why, when we dug a hole in our backyard to plant a tree, we found vast amounts of sand. In astonishment, we excavated shovelful after shovelful, just a couple of inches below the surface of unassuming scraggly lawn. Even though we live at least forty miles from the shore of Lake Michigan—our nearest source of sand—we found ourselves, suddenly, at the beach.

3. Contents

During our last move, I sifted through a box I had not touched in a decade, the layers geologic strata, going deeper into the past the farther down I went—the kids' old drawings and birthday cards, notes addressed to *Mom* and *Mommy* and then *MOMY*, growth charts, a set of hospital identification bands, one with my name, the other labeled *Baby Boy*, then, further down, another set, my own and *Baby Girl*. I kept excavating, into my pre-motherhood life, finding old essays and certificates of long-forgotten achievements, until at the bottom, I came upon what looked like more hospital bracelets, which puzzled me, but when I read the names on them, *Nellie Stevens Holly, Fat Albert Blue Spruce, Acer Saccharum,* I recognized them: tags from the trees I planted twenty years and six houses and four states ago. The box, curated by accident, contained the records of creatures I've nurtured in the world. Google Maps Street View took me to my old neighborhood to see again my three trees, and I was reassured that they were thriving, filling the front yard, shading the blank brick face of the house, the sugar maple not yet ready to tap—my dream—but getting there. All of them have outgrown their nursery bracelets, just as the kids have. The bands that once encircled their minuscule ankles might fit around their thumbs now. I told them about all this, but they were unamazed. They only said, "Of course, Mom. You've always loved trees." And the proof is already in our new backyard, where my latest progeny—a white oak and a catalpa—wait for spring to unfurl their tender leaves.

Porcupine Mountains Wilderness State Park

THE NIGHT FOLLOWS CLOSE

Day full-blown and splendid—day of the immense
sun, action, ambition, laughter,
The Night follows close with millions of suns,
and sleep and restoring darkness.
—WALT WHITMAN

Porcupine Mountains Wilderness State Park, Michigan
Summer 2022

I. Darkness

We arrive on the summer solstice, the day yawning so wide with light we aren't awake when it begins or ends. From the first night of my three-week residency, the boy has no trouble going right to sleep even before dusk ends, while slumber evades me. All night I have shallow, fitful dreams about electronic devices: misplacing my phone, forgetting my phone, my laptop not starting, my batteries dying, my connections to my digital life failing. I don't even have my laptop with me, and my phone, useless without a signal, is off. Still, my devices haunt me in the unfamiliar darkness.

"It was light so late, and then it was so, so dark," I write the next morning. And on my second morning: "Another restless night." I discover the logbook in which past artists who have stayed in the cabin left their handwritten musings. "The woods here are ancient, and night and silence fall over you like a heavy blanket," wrote Leigh Cox in 2016. "The first two nights I struggled to sleep, leaving the gas light on, playing music from my phone, anything to take the edge off being alone in these penetrating woods." It's some comfort that I'm not alone in my deep-night aloneness.

"Two-thirds of the world's population—including 99 percent of people living in the continental United States and western Europe—

no longer experience a truly dark sky, a night untouched by artificial electric light," writes Paul Bogard in *The End of Night: Searching for Natural Darkness in an Age of Artificial Light*. In *Healing Night: The Science and Spirit of Sleeping, Dreaming, and Awakening*, Rubin R. Naiman writes that 10 percent of Earth's population has compromised night vision due to urban glow, and 40 percent of the U.S. population never experiences conditions dark enough for human eyes to adapt to night vision, adding: "I believe that the majority of us suffer from a chronic darkness deficiency."

Night-sky enthusiasts have been decrying light pollution and singing the praises of darkness for decades. In 2001 Geoff Chester of the U.S. Naval Observatory called the night sky "the world's largest national park," while Dan Duriscoe, an environmental scientist who pioneered night sky protection for the National Park Service, believes that preserving night sky is "an integral part of the wilderness ethic." A 2007 declaration adopted by UNESCO and the World Tourism Organization called "an unpolluted" night sky "an inalienable right of humankind." And yet, a truly dark sky has become a rarity, in many cases accessible only to those with the means to travel to remote places.

My sky in the Porcupine Mountains is not even optimum darkness. On the Bortle scale, which is used to evaluate night sky brightness from a 9 (inner-city sky) to a 1 (excellent dark sky), that elusive Class 1 sky is like a unicorn. According to Bogard, "many question if such a sky still exists in the Lower 48. While rumors arrive from the deserts of eastern Oregon and southern Utah, the Nebraska prairie and the Texas-Mexico border, there's no denying that Bortle has described a level of darkness that for most of human history was common but for the modern Western world has become unreal." Later, while looking at a Bortle map online, I will discover that my Upper Peninsula sky is Class 2, a "typical truly dark site." Good, but not "excellent." Still, it's much darker than the small city where I now live in Indiana or the one in which I grew up in Southern California, both of them designated as Class 7, "suburban/urban transition." The city in Russia where I was born is also Class 7. In fact, as I digitally soar around the world, I will discover that the majority of the other places that I've called home—in Virginia, Nebraska, Connecticut—are Class 7.

Wide awake in the middle of my fourth night, I go outside to visit the outhouse, and I'm instantly stunned by the depth of the darkness. "What the other artists wrote is no lie: it is DARK here," I write the next day. "This has to be the darkest place I've ever been—the deep, dark woods of fairy tales. There is almost no sky, due to the trees." And there's no moon that I can see. I don't even know where to look for it, what phase it's in. I'm estranged from the night sky.

Sandra Lee Starck, who lived in the cabin in 2010, explains it to me in her logbook entry:

> Living in this river valley—particularly one that has a high ridge to the south—one does not get any FULL MOON view at this time of year!!!—it's behind the mountain! Come winter this valley will be *filled* with moonlight—but now, near summer solstice, the moon is in such a southern position that it does not make it high in the sky enough to illuminate the valley. I had arrived, anticipating a beautiful full moon in the forest! NOT TO BE!! And now as the moon is nearly a crescent (and still way south) it is the storybook BLACK night, so BLACK you can't see your hand in front of your face BLACK. I LOVE IT!!!

When Sherrie, the Friends of the Porkies volunteer in charge of the artist-in-residence program, first brought us to the cabin, she left us with a warning: "It gets dark here. If you're going to be out late, bring a flashlight with you to find your way back to the cabin." I had nodded, without understanding, in the manner of the uninitiated. Sherrie knew what she was talking about. She had spent decades in these woods, had helped to erect this timber frame cabin for artists fifteen years ago. She knew about night in the Porkies.

That first week in the cabin, as I read the words of the artists who have come before me, as I begin to apprehend the contours of darkness, I think about banishment—how we have banished dark, cold, damp, hunger, thirst, all of the discomforts of the wild, believing we have triumphed, not realizing how we have impoverished ourselves in the process. To come to wilderness is to reacquaint ourselves with some of what we've excised from our lives. Bugs, for example. The dark. Night is another wilderness that we have pushed to the margins.

It's not just artists who come to live in these forests. The Porkies offer visitors an extensive network of rustic cabins that date back to the 1940s and 1950s. These cabins have their own logbooks where visitors record their thoughts. I discover this history when I find in my cabin bookcase a volume published in 2001 titled *The Porcupine Wilderness Journals* that compiles highlights from many of these logbooks. Here, in these pages, are other people who have communed with the darkness.

On June 12, 1975, Doug F. wrote, "Do you know how black it is when you shut your eyes inside a closed closet? Well, it was the same way here last night. It didn't matter if your eyes were open or shut, you saw the same thing—absolutely nothing. Joe said it scared him when he first woke up during the night. He thought he had gone blind from drinking the river water!"

On September 23, 1980, an unknown visitor wrote, "New worlds are seen through the widened pupils of the night. Thoughts, like shooting stars, emerge and glisten in all corners of the sky. Some live only as long as an initial spark—others take the unlikely turns of a cedar's roots upon a rock."

Darkness is not a monolithic state. Just as there are many qualities to light, there are many qualities to darkness. And yet, because our sense of sight dominates, at least for the sighted among us, we relegate any experience of darkness to a single category. "When we see images of deep caves or megalithic recesses we can only do so because of camera flashes and other artificial means of lighting," writes Robert Hensey in *The Archaeology of Darkness.* "What we are actually photographing is the temporary removal of darkness. Darkness is the opposite of 'illumination', enlightenment—and all those other light-oriented words we rely on so heavily to describe understanding; the dark is where the unseen, unformed and misunderstood things abide, that which has not been examined in the cold hard light of day." Darkness is the antithesis of image—at least in its visual sense. Darkness eludes our ability to capture it. We assume there's nothing there. Then we shine a light on it, annihilating it, and declare it empty, a negation.

I begin to wonder: What if, rather than being a diminished state, darkness is an enhanced state wherein we access subterranean parts of ourselves? What if darkness is not the absence of light, but rather light is the absence of darkness? What if we can be endarkened, just as we can be enlightened? Whatever is happening to me in the Porkies feels like an endarkening.

II. Illumination

We now speak of *nature-deficit disorder* and *environmental generational amnesia* and *shifting baseline syndrome.* We have created many terms to talk about what happens to us when we are cut off from the wild. "If you have never known a night sky any darker than the one you have now, why would you think anything is wrong?" asks Bogard. If you have never seen the Milky Way, how do you know what you're missing?

There is an apocryphal story about the 1994 Northridge earthquake: When Los Angeles lost power, emergency centers and even the Griffith Observatory received numerous calls from frightened people reporting a "giant silvery cloud" over the city. That mysterious cloud was, of course, our very own Milky Way Galaxy. "A luminous fog now smothers a quarter of the earth's surface and is thick enough in many places to blot out the stars," writes Ed Yong in *An Immense World.* Eighty percent of North Americans can no longer see the Milky Way. Our own night sky has become foreign to us.

Meanwhile, our artificial lights grow ever brighter; just observe the gas station/food mart/rest stop oases on interstates that are illuminated as bright as operating theaters. "As our surroundings grow brighter, we grow used to that level of brightness, and so anything dimmer seems extraordinarily dim, even dark," writes Bogard. In other words, we have exchanged our view of the Milky Way for a well-lit strip mall. "Sensory pollution is the pollution of disconnection," Yong writes. "It detaches us from the cosmos. It drowns out the stimuli that link animals to their surroundings and to each other."

When I assigned a portion of Richard Louv's *Last Child in the Woods: Saving Our Children from Nature-Deficit Disorder* to my college writing students in 2015, many of them nodded along in agreement with Louv's message. "Oh, yeah," they said. "He's totally right. When I was a kid, we used to play outdoors, but now, kids don't go outside anymore." They told anecdotes about younger siblings, cousins, kids they babysat. "But do you realize," I asked them, "that this book was published ten years ago, when you were children? Do you realize that *you* are the children Louv was writing about?" They shook their heads. No, this wasn't true of them. They went outdoors plenty. "How do you even know what you're missing?" I asked them. They stared back at me. "How do *I* know?" I added, thinking of my own 1980s suburban childhood, the prophecies that foretold a doom brought on by too many TV shows and videogames.

In *The Outermost House,* Henry Beston writes:

> With lights and ever more lights, we drive the holiness and beauty of night back to the forests and the sea; the little villages, the crossroads even, will have none of it. Are modern folk, perhaps, afraid of night? Do they fear that vast serenity, the mystery of infinite space, the austerity of stars? Having made themselves at home in a civilization obsessed with power, which explains its whole world in terms of energy, do they fear at night for their dull acquiescence and the pattern of their belief? Be the answer what it will, to-day's civilization is full of people who have not the slightest notion of the character or the poetry of night, who have never even seen night.

Were it not for his slightly dated language, we might suppose Beston is a contemporary of ours, but he is not. A naturalist, Beston lived in a cottage on the dunes of Cape Cod in the mid-1920s, publishing his book about his experience in 1928. Even a century ago, he recognized the detrimental effects of artificial light. He recognized, long before many others, that we were losing the night.

Thomas Edison, who is probably as responsible as any individual can be for the electrification of the world, was a man who scorned sleep. He wrote, "Most people overeat 100 percent and oversleep 100 percent. The extra 100 percent makes them unhealthy and inefficient. The person who sleeps eight or ten hours a night is never fully asleep and never fully awake." Famous for taking brief "cat naps" in his lab, he also said, "Everything which decreases the sum total of man's sleep, increases the sum total of man's capabilities. There is really no reason why men should go to bed at all."

Perhaps it was not only his incandescent lightbulb but also his unrelenting work ethic that contributed to creating our 24/7 consumerist culture. With the constant, grinding work of his labs—he tested hundreds, perhaps thousands, of filaments before finding one that worked—he had an assembly line mentality; dogged determination and ceaseless work drove him forward. He was a man who battled the enemies of sleep and darkness, who believed in breakneck progress, technology and innovation moving ever forward, consequences be damned.

As electrification spread its tentacles out from the urban centers into rural areas, those who lived in the deep, dark countryside eventually witnessed the wonder of illumination. That moment when electricity was connected to a house came to be known as "zero hour." As Jane Brox describes in *Brilliant: The Evolution of Artificial Light*, "The first thing some did once they were hooked up was to turn on every light and then drive down the road just to look back at their illuminated house." It must have felt like a miracle.

III. Wakefulness

I start waking in the night and listening to the darkness: the scritch of an animal, the song of our river, fluctuating from a soft sibilation to a barreling roar, depending on recent rainfall. Lucid but subdued, I rise, put on shoes, slip from the cabin to wander the forest. Life teems among the stately hemlocks: the thrum and whine of insects, the dark rustlings among plants, the delicate wake of a flying creature cleaving the air, the sudden twitch and scamper of a being I can't see.

These hemlocks are the trees of fairy tales. In the cabin I find a 1981 copy of *Michigan Trees* and pore over the entry on eastern hemlock, learning that mature trees form "a massive, pyramidal, ragged crown of densely foliated branches." They are "highly shade tolerant; very slow-growing; very long-lived (600+ years)," and they "may exist 50–100 years or more in the shaded forest understory and gradually reach the overstory." A hemlock tree, once established, "creates its own microclimate."

It's among these giants that I prowl every night; I live in their world. Each night, I wander the perimeter of our cabin, absorbing the darkness, apprehending the night, drinking it in through all my senses, and then I return to the cabin and go back to sleep until morning.

In his meticulously researched history of the night, *At Day's Close: Night in Times Past*, A. Roger Ekirch describes a phenomenon that he calls segmented sleep. "Until the close of the early modern era, Western Europeans on most evenings experienced two major intervals of sleep bridged by up to an hour or more of quiet wakefulness," he writes. Night was bifurcated into "first sleep" and "second sleep," linked by a period of alertness during which people would socialize, read, or "ponder visions in the dead of night," among other things. Ekirch calls these late-night wakeful periods "our oldest path to the human psyche."

What we now consider "normal" sleep—an unbroken eight-hour stretch—is, in fact, a relatively recent development. "Sleeping in one straight shot through the night—'consolidated' sleep—has become a near-universal expectation, even for those whose bodies and minds seem naturally inclined to shut down and switch back on differently," writes Benjamin Reiss in *Wild Nights: How Taming Sleep Created Our Restless World*. "Would-be sleepers are encouraged to develop rigid bedtime routines, regardless of season or setting. Sleep is supposed to occur in a private and almost neurotically sealed space, with, at most, two consenting adults sharing a bed." Before coming to the Porkies, before finding my sleep broken in two with a period of nighttime lucidity, I had never questioned the gold standard of consolidated sleep.

For a class on the history of the English language, my older child D. once wrote a paper on the history of the word *blind*. "When describing a place or object, *blind* meant that the subject was dark or dim; for example, a candle might be said to be blind if it was only emitting dim light," they wrote, continuing:

> In Old and Middle English, we see *blind* as a word which means "lack of sight," but it does not seem to function as a discrete identity category in the same way it does now. There are permanently blind people, of course, but because places and things can also be blind, there is a fluidity in the term. This omnipresent relationship between light and sight bestows a transient quality on even literal designations of blindness; when a place is poorly lit, you are blind, in a blind place. When light returns, you cease to be blind. There is an implied blamelessness here—to be blind means to be destitute of sight, but the failure to see might not be in the seer's physical inability to see but rather in the environment or object's failure to be seeable.

This understanding of *blind* feels more capacious to me. In the Porkies, I was blind in a blind wood. The condition was mutual and temporary, rooted in a particular experience, not in a permanent state or identity. Our modern conception of blindness limits the range of experiences the word once encompassed. To place blindness wholly within the eyes, to define it as a mechanical failure of the body, banishes other kinds of blindness from our understanding of ourselves and the world.

In the Porkies, the rigid demarcations between sleeping and wakefulness, between self and other, are growing more porous.

A creature who lives between the shingles of our cabin's roof sometimes gnaws and scratches in the night, rousing me to nighttime lucidity. The membrane of the cabin—the skin that protects my human world from the wilderness outside—seems so thin. I rise and go out, answering the call of the darkness.

Roaming in the forest late at night, I think of my teenaged, night-wandering self of three decades ago. During my California summer nights, after gorging on MTV and Nintendo, I would go outside and wander, lingering in the corners of darkness, bathing under the orange glow of suburban streetlights. I craved transgressions of all kinds—cigarettes, alcohol, stoner boys—and constantly pushed back on what felt like the narrowly circumscribed boundaries of my life. Night was a time to evade scrutiny, to roam free, to feel my feral self come into her own. Some nights I walked the empty streets to Box Springs, my beautiful sleeping mountain range, draped on the edge of my neighborhood like a fallen giant. I imagined her always as a woman, buxom and curved, and her body was dark—dark dark dark like velvet, studded with boulders that pearled under the moon, with the city spreading out around, casting its jeweled light. I lay on the body of the mountain, draped my head over a boulder, imagined the jewels of the city crowning me. Sometimes, I saw the shape of a coyote moving in the darkness. I drank it all in, this life in the shadowlands, satisfying a deep craving for night during those final years before I took up permanent residence in the adult realm and acquiesced to its demands. I always came down from the mountains and returned to my own yard before the sun rose. Sometimes, as dawn rimmed the edges of the sky, I would hide in the bushes and watch my father leave for work. One dawn, I stared directly into his eyes as he stood in the kitchen drinking coffee and peering out at the yard, but he didn't seem to see me, and I understood why: because I hadn't yet returned from the night. I hadn't reassumed my human form.

For four years in the mid-1970s, right after they were married, my parents lived in separate places—my father in the United States, my mother in the Soviet Union. During that time, my mother most often wrote to my father at night, the only time that was truly hers. She scorned sleep because there was always so much to do—books to read, music to listen to, thoughts to have—but also, she had to wrest time away from her daytime demands of teaching at the university, writing her dissertation, caring for a young child. *I write from deep night,* she often began, alternating back and forth between her native Russian and her limited English. The word for *deep* in Russian also means *profound,* and when she wrote in English, she used the latter word. *I write to you from profound night.* I prefer this translation. And in those long, profound nights, she wrote and wrote.

Soon the night will end, and I am still writing a letter to you, but this is so wonderful—to remember you and to talk to you at least mentally. I have a feeling that with every letter we penetrate one another more deeply. No one has ever understood me as well as you. And it seems to me to be a real miracle that you understand me better and better, that no limits to this understanding appear—it's as though your soul is boundless in its love for me. My need to see you, talk to you, be with you is now more important than everything else in the world. It is already getting light. The night is ending. I need to sleep at least two or three hours. Forgive me for ending this letter. I would like to talk with you endlessly.

This is maybe my very earliest perception of life: I remember one of the adults said, "The sun has risen." I was interested in seeing how it had risen and what this meant. Of course, I imagined this sun in a very concrete way. It is likely that it was winter because I was not allowed to go outside. I remember that I walked into the other room where the sun was touching the walls. And when I approached the window, I couldn't see what was going on outside—the window was too high—but suddenly I saw how a bright pink light splashed on the window. The windows were covered in dew or frost patterns, but the light passing through them was so bright that I squinted. This was my first perception of the sun and light. I remember that the strong warmth coming from the window was connected with a feeling of some kind of life warmth and happiness. Later, Mama told me, as she was leaving, that I will lie down and go to sleep when night comes. I began to wait. And you know, I thought that a real live creature that called itself "night" would come, and then I could go to sleep. Of course, no one came, only the windows became black. When Mama came back, I was sitting by the window and waiting for night to come. How great was my amazement when I found out that the blackness outside the windows was in fact night.

The only thing that made sleep worthwhile for my mother was the promise that she might see my father in her dreams. *You come to me in my dreams at night; I am grateful to fate for my dream glimpses of you.* In dozens of letters, she reports on her dream visions. *I saw you tonight in my dreams. You were holding my hands in yours—this was such a delight—also because I saw your face—your extraordinary face.* She remained a creature of the night, even after moving to the United States and being reunited with my father. I always had the impression that she lived her real, vital life in the night, that she expended her night energies on my father, on herself, on her deepest thinking and feeling, and that the mother I knew was a faded, diminished self, exhibiting a flatness and weariness as she faced the tedium of daytime life.

One late night, reading by the light of a gas lamp, I discover in the cabin's logbook a poem written by 2012 artist-in-residence Francis Kazemek. He wrote about standing in a clearing beneath hemlocks, looking at a starry sky. Perhaps, I think, he had rested in this very chair to compose these lines. The membrane of time that separates us—just ten years—feels so thin, so permeable, that I nearly sense him in the room with me. "Stars glitter a kind of hope," the poem concludes, "For something I can't imagine."

I go out and look up at the stars burning in the deep lake of sky between trees, feeling the same hope for something I can't imagine. Or maybe I can imagine it, and it is just this: to stand with hope beneath stars. Maybe that is all many of us want, in an age when hope is in short supply, when apocalypse feels nascent. Maybe we don't need to know what the hope is for but only that it is possible.

IV. Dreamers

When my children were small, we often planned to meet in our dreams. "Where do you want to meet tonight?" one of them would ask as I was tucking them in. We would agree on a place—the beach at Hammonasset, a peak in the Box Springs Mountains, the ruin of Cair Paravel in Narnia, a Russian birch forest near the hut of Baba Yaga. My children, who shared a room then, would tell elaborate stories about the train that they would ride on their journey to sleep, what would happen once they arrived in their dreams. Of course, we never all managed to arrive at our designated location, but the point was in possibility, in dreaming of our dreams in advance.

Maurice Sendak's dreamworlds and nighttime journeys—*Where the Wild Things Are, In the Night Kitchen, Outside Over There*—were loved and feared by my children. In childhood, we live with a keener awareness of darkness and night, of our night selves, of the deeply symbolic language of dreams. Nightmares and night terrors are common. A baby sister kidnapped by goblins in the dark of night, a boy who dons a wolf suit and sails to an island to romp with wild creatures, another boy who falls naked through his dream into a night kitchen where he is nearly baked into a cake: these are all the fabric of childhood dreams, which often balance precariously between delight and terror.

I vividly recall a night terror I experienced at the age of four or five, when my parents and I still lived with my paternal grandparents. Sleeping in my aunt Susan's old bedroom on an antique chaise longue upholstered in lavender satin, I recall the terror of being trapped in an indeterminate realm between waking and sleeping as a hideous wolflike monster attempted to devour me. I was lucid enough to have a murky awareness of my surroundings—my mother and grandmother trying to wrench me out of my terror, my desperate scrabbling at the lavender fabric, my uncontrollable sobbing and screaming—yet my true self was trapped behind a scrim, inside my own vision, which felt like the real, throbbing, monstrous world. I had been turned inside out: my monster world was the real one, and the one in which hands were gripping me and trying to rattle me awake was the dream world. My two protectors, the denizens of the waking world, were strangers, intruders, taking me away from who I really was, from the horror of a monster that had sprung up in my own mind. Slowly, they pulled me out of the depths, saving me from my nighttime self. Reserved and exhausted upon my return, I did not feel grateful for their rescue. Forever after I felt changed—a feeling that faded but never disappeared.

In the cabin, I listen to my boy sleep, but his rest is placid, undisturbed. He is beyond the realm of childhood, when his mind was so permeable to darkness. At fourteen, he's soundly sleeping his way to adulthood.

We go backpacking for four days, and when we return to the cabin, my aunt Olga starts coming to me in my dreams. It's always the same: She's running through the forest, and I'm following her, struggling to keep up. Sometimes, we're running through a Russian forest on the outskirts of Samara where both she and I were born, sometimes we're running through the forests of the Upper Peninsula, and sometimes I can't tell where we are because I'm so desperate to not lose sight of her as she darts among the trees that I can't apprehend my surroundings. Most of the time, she runs in the nude, barefoot, svelte, and self-possessed as a wild animal, while I lumber clumsily behind, wearing unsuitable clothing that trips me and snags on branches. In every dream, no matter how fast I run, I lose her to the wild, the dark.

I knew Olga, my mother's younger and only sister, in the first three years of my life, and later, during my Russian summers when we went back to visit. Olga smoldered with intensity, her penetrating gaze boring into me, her questions probing the depths of our existence. Why do we live? How do we live? How is the human animal different from other members of the animal kingdom? She was a voracious seeker of meaning. Art was her religion. She devoured books—Herman Hesse, Mikhail Bulgakov, Goethe, Carlos Castaneda—and especially music. Listening to Verdi on her scratchy record player, smoking unfiltered cigarettes, she would get a remote, rapturous look in her eyes as she stared straight past me, at some vision I couldn't see, reaching for some orgasm of the mind. *There! There!* she would cry. *Did you hear it?*

Outspoken and honest to the point of rudeness, she always said what she thought, eschewing politeness and small talk. As a child, she chalked anti-Soviet sentiments on the sidewalk; as a young adult, she walked the streets wearing jean shorts and smoking, indifferent to the old women, the babushkas, who chided her for indecency. Her quiet and stoic parents, who had suffered through Stalin's purges and the unimaginable bloodshed of the Russian twentieth century, looked upon their daughter in horror; they had learned that there is a chasm as wide as death between what you think and what you say. Olga, born five years after Stalin's death, had disdain for her parents—for their meekness, their unquestioning acceptance of the drudgery of Soviet life. Conflict crackled between them for years—especially since even in adulthood, Olga had to keep living at home. As a single woman, she was not eligible for her own apartment in the Soviet Union. And she would never marry, because she was involved with an older married man, Dzhon, with whom she carried on a decades-long affair. *You may walk completely nude in front of your husband,* she informed me one summer, and by *husband* she meant her mate for life.

Olga told her fortune in elaborate rituals, divining the future in cards and by staring into the murky depths of mirrors facing one another to glimpse the amorphous shape of what was to come. Despite her mystical leanings, she also had a scientific mind. Trained as a biologist, she saw human beings as members of the animal kingdom, as organisms worthy of scientific study. Her love of animals knew no bounds; she filled that small Soviet apartment with mice, cats, dogs, canaries, even hissing cockroaches. She also loved the outdoors. In the summers, she often spent weeks at the family's dacha, a rustic shack on a plot of land where my grandparents gardened and cultivated fruit trees. She loved her solitude. Being alone with her own mind gave her the deepest pleasure.

And she luxuriated in sleep. *I am going to go sleep now,* she would announce, with joy and anticipation, and then she would disappear for hours. Her long sleeps often happened during the day, because her nighttime hours were devoted to reading and listening to music and rapturing. For Olga, sleeping was not a waste of time, a necessary banality. Rather, sleep held the promise of insight. Upon waking, Olga recounted her dreams with the care and seriousness that she gave to the events of her waking life. She read her dreams like auguries that held portents and wisdom.

The boundary between actually being in the forest and dreaming of being in the forest starts to dissolve. In my bifurcated night, I rise and go outside during my watchful time. During my sleeping time, I'm still in the forest, trailing my aunt, who is leading me somewhere, if only I could keep up, if only I could overcome my daytime self and claim my wild, night self. She's leading me to the real darkness, the very heart of night, where she has made her permanent home. But every time she outruns me.

Beston tells us that night "is the other half of the day's tremendous wheel." The poet Bill Yake writes that "half the forest is night." Georg Christoph Lichtenberg, a German physicist of the eighteenth century, observes, "Our entire history is only the history of waking man." In other words, we are missing half the story.

"Sleep would seem to be resistant to literary treatment, because nothing 'happens' while we sleep, and in a sense we're not even 'there' to have anything happen to us," writes Reiss. But what if, just as darkness is not merely an absence of light, sleep is not an absence of consciousness, a swath of empty, lost time? My entire history has been a history of my waking self. What if I endeavored to tell the story of my nighttime self? I wouldn't know where to begin.

When I teach fiction in my introductory creative writing class, I stipulate my students must write a *realistic* short story, adding the alliterative addendum: "no dogs, no dreams, no drugs!" I explain that I don't want a story with a tired twist ending—which so many novice writers believe to be clever—in which on the fifth page of a six-page story, we discover that the narrator is actually on drugs, or is dreaming, or is a dog, all of which could effortlessly explain away any weirdness or plot incongruities. I tell my students I don't want to become emotionally invested in characters whose story is built on deceit. And besides, dreamworlds (whether produced by a sleeping, hallucinating, or canine mind) do not follow the rules of fiction, which are the rules of cause and effect. As E. M. Forster famously declared, *the king died and then the queen died* is merely a story, whereas *the king died and then the queen died of grief* is a plot. Narratives of dream states tend to be a string of unconnected events—this happened, and then this happened, and then this happened—with no cause and effect. What we want in fiction, I tell my students, is plot.

I wonder, though, if my impatience for dream states is actually a resistance to altered states of consciousness, a prejudice for the logical and rational. "Poetry is as necessary to comprehension as science," writes Beston, who sees science as a realm of the day and poetry as a realm of the night. These are words to live by, yet so often—most of the time—my own writing is dominated by the rational, the empirical. Perhaps poetry, more than any other genre, is the most direct conduit to our dream selves, and the fact that I am not a poet shows my affinity for the light of day. Since I shed off my teenage rebellion, since I eschewed darkness to become an adult, I am no longer at home in the night world.

During one of my Russian summers, maybe 1984 or 1987, when I was nine or twelve and all of us (three generations) lived in that two-room apartment, I remember being up one night, not fully awake, wandering the rooms. I moved around the foldout beds, the sleeping mounds of flesh that felt so remote to me, then came into the kitchen, and there she was. Olga. She sat on a stool at the small table, perfectly still, her luminous eyes filling her face, looking into me deeply but also looking through me, like she was there but not there. She was her night self, and I was my night self, and we said nothing. We met that way in a mutual dream, our private night place—a place where we don't normally encounter others. We communed in the kitchen, night soul with night soul, and then I went back past the sleeping bodies, back to my rickety cot, and I didn't remember any of this until I was in the Porkies, until Olga started seeping into my dreams, until our night selves started to meet, until I realized that she was someone who always perceived her reality as through the filter of a dream, reading her life as deeply symbolic and strange and luminous.

In college, I spent many hours in the darkroom doing black-and-white photography. It's an irony, perhaps, that in order to create objects for viewing—images—we went into the darkness where we could not see. I am not thinking of the room where I made prints from negatives, where there was a weak red light to see by, but rather of the utter blackness of the cramped space where I removed the film from my camera and deposited it by feel into the canister in which I developed it.

Olga, too, dabbled in photography. There was no darkroom in the apartment, so when she was removing film from her camera, she would climb into the heavy wooden wardrobe, and her mother would lock her in, since there was no way of latching the door from the inside. One time, Olga told me, her mother locked her in and went to the kitchen, where she started cooking, and forgot all about Olga, who was trapped in among the winter coats, muffled and screaming, separated from her mother by the massive walls of Stalin-era architecture. Once she conquered her claustrophobia, though, the darkness astonished her. She plunged through layers of darkness, each one darker than the last. For what felt like hours, she fell into profound darkness, and when her mother finally remembered her and let her out, Olga was enraged at the interruption, insulted by the blinding light, averse to returning to the illuminated world. She couldn't believe that long, luxurious plunge into darkness could be undone in an instant, at the turn of a key.

Later, after the Soviet Union fell, after my grandfather died, Olga had a child, my cousin Margarita. Later still, after my grandmother died, after Margarita got older, Olga started going on long expeditions into the Zhiguli Mountains, Samara Bend National Park, the wild areas around Samara. After Dzhon died, after Margarita moved into her own apartment, Olga grew more and more enamored of the wilderness. She remained fiercely independent, adoring her solitude, forging her own way.

One night, I dream I'm a tree. I gaze upon the cabin with a new horror, seeing it for what it really is: made of the flesh of fallen kin, death and murder on display. But immediately upon having this thought, my understanding shifts, and I realize I'm not an *I* at all, that trees do not interpret the world in personal ways, that they grow out of the compost of the forest floor, a place of birth and death commingling. They don't worry for their dignity or their souls. They don't shudder at the sight of downed wood. Rather, they live in the cycle of life and death from which we struggle with all our might to extricate ourselves.

In another dream, the trees are on the move, shifting in the darkness of the night, pulling up their roots and dragging them to new locations, speaking to one another in deep, gravelly voices in a register so low it's all but inaudible to human ears. I stare wide-eyed into the night to see where they are going, but the lumbering dark shapes of craggy giants are nearly invisible in the darkness. Straining to hear their mutterings, I understand nothing.

And always, deep in the blind wood, Olga slips through the trees.

In the spring of 2020, Olga had a vivid dream that she related to Margarita: She was standing in the forest with a mountain before her when she heard Dzhon's voice emanating from behind the mountain, calling to her, but she refused to answer him. Suddenly, the phone that she was holding in her hands began to ring, and the caller ID read *Dzhon*. Then Olga's mother walked up to her and said, "Answer the phone. Dzhon is calling you." But Olga did not answer the phone, and then she woke up. At the time, she read the dream to mean that she was to go on living, since she did not listen to the advice of her deceased mother or answer the call of her dead lover. But shortly thereafter, she did answer the call. Olga died during our pandemic summer in a COVID hospital in Samara at the age of sixty-two.

V. Illumination

As someone who has always lived with easy access to the comforts of modern civilization—shelter, heat, light, food, water—I cannot claim to know what life was like in earlier times, nor would I ever say that we would be better off without artificial light. "The dark was, for all of human existence, a palpable and universal obstacle to human happiness," writes Ernest Freeberg in *The Age of Edison: Electric Light and the Invention of Modern America.* "Throughout history, to be in darkness was to be diminished, shuttered from the world." I cannot disagree.

And yet, there is a pernicious link between the hunger for illumination of the Industrial Age and the dark side of capitalism. Freeberg explains:

> Some friends of the working class predicted that electric light, which seemed to promise middle-class consumers nothing but pleasure and convenience, would only bring further misery to the working class. Forced by poverty to work whenever bosses offered them the chance, and even to send their children into the factories, these industrial workers found some small measure of protection in the darkness, the one time when the 'taskmaster' could not demand their toil. Now a flood of inexpensive artificial light into fields and factories threatened to erase this natural, God-given safeguard against exploitation.

Artificial light meant workers could labor around the clock, no longer finding liberty in darkness.

In *24/7: Late Capitalism and the End of Sleep,* Jonathan Crary writes of the ways in which contemporary capitalism has commodified and exploited every basic necessity—hunger, thirst, sexual desire, even friendship—with the exception of sleep. Crary argues that sleep—with its lack of productivity, its passivity, its profound remoteness from our connected consumer lives—is one realm that stubbornly resists commodification. "Sleep is an uncompromising interruption of the theft of time from us by capitalism."

Capitalism, though, has certainly tried to steal sleep from us—through artificially illuminated nights, through the alluring promise of glowing screens, through the standardization and consolidation of sleep. Capitalism steals sleep from us and then sells it back in the form of drugs, teas, supplements, sleep aids, self-help books, therapy. We can see examples of this elsewhere: the corporations that peddle carcinogens in products emblazoned with pink cancer awareness ribbons, selling both the disease and a promise of its cure.

In 1916 Edison started going on camping expeditions with his industrial tycoon buddies Henry Ford and Harvey Firestone, accompanied by the naturalist John Burroughs. Freeberg writes:

> Edison joined the growing movement of Americans who longed for something missing in their hectic urban lives, something that might be restored if they could only get "back to nature and rough it in the wilderness." "I don't want to be near electricity," Edison explained to reporters. "An old suit, an old hat, a few French novels and the fishing rod, that's all I bother with." Touring the Adirondacks, his "gypsy" band of celebrity industrialists searched for the small dirt roads where they hoped to avoid all those other touring motorists who shared this desire for a less hectic, rural way of life. Edison described his annual escape into the woods as his "feeble protest against civilization."

He might be said to have been seeking an escape from the very civilization he helped to create.

"Sleep disorders are the most prevalent health concern in America and probably the rest of the industrialized world today," writes Naiman. And light at night—especially the blue light of screens—inhibits our ability to produce melatonin, which in turn interferes with our sleep. Poor sleep has been linked with a host of health issues, including obesity, viral infections, heart disease, all types of cancer. It might not be much of an exaggeration to say that artificial light is killing us.

And the lure of screens—which promise news, entertainment, companionship, fulfillment—is powerful indeed. Information overload—be it through the channels of telegraphs and daily printed newspapers of the nineteenth century or the 24/7 internet news cycle and doomscrolling of the modern age—has been a threat to sleeping and dreaming for over a century. Indeed, as far back as the seventeenth century, when empiricism and scientific thinking began to hold sway, the dream life started to fade from prominence.

"For all the cultural diversity in how dreams were understood from antiquity into the 1500s, there is nonetheless a near-universal acceptance of dreaming as integral to the lives of individuals and communities," writes Crary. "Only from the seventeenth century does this singular element of sleeping begin to be marginalized and discredited. Dreaming cannot be accommodated within conceptions of mental life based on empirical sense perception or on abstract rational thought."

Banishing our dreams to the realm of the irrational and insignificant, viewing them as "a mere self-regulatory adjustment of the sensory overload of waking life" that has "neurochemical explanations," as Crary writes, we explain away our luminous nighttime selves as a wacky side-effect of brain circuitry, mere detritus that our waking selves shrug off.

Visionary writers of dystopian fiction have been expressing our anxieties about artificial illumination and the hijacking of our sleep and dreams for well over a century. Yevgeny Zamyatin's *We*, written in 1920–21 following the Russian Revolution of 1917, portrays a society built on logic and mathematical precision in which dreaming has been completely eliminated. When the unnamed narrator experiences a dream, he concludes he must be ill. "I have never dreamed before," he reports in his journal, continuing:

> They say that with the ancients dreaming was a perfectly ordinary, normal occurrence. But of course, their whole life was a dreadful

> whirling carousel—green, orange, Buddhas, sap. We, however, know that dreams are a serious psychic disease. And I know that until this moment my brain has been a chronometrically exact gleaming mechanism without a single speck of dust. But now . . . Yes, precisely: I feel some alien body in my brain, like the finest eyelash in the eye.

That he feels his dream state to be an intrusion from the outside reveals the degree to which society has suppressed irrational, individual desires. Dreams are dangerous—a "disease" that must be eradicated—because they represent an internal wilderness beyond the control of the state.

Aldous Huxley's *Brave New World*, published in 1932, envisions a society that adheres to Fordism—as in Henry Ford—which is built on the principles of the assembly line (standardization, consumerism, mass production). Human beings are engineered in artificial wombs to belong to predetermined classes, and much of their conditioning is done via hypnopaedia, or "sleep-teaching." Through all of their sleeping hours, children hear the same messages repeated, hundreds and thousands of times over years, until they are fully internalized, "till at last the child's mind *is* these suggestions, and the sum of the suggestions *is* the child's mind," as the director of the Central London Hatchery and Conditioning Centre explains. "And not the child's mind only. The adult's mind too—all his life long. The mind that judges and desires and decides—made up of these suggestions." In a society where unorthodoxy is the greatest threat, the realm of sleep has been fully colonized for propaganda and brainwashing.

Unrelenting artificial light is another concern of dystopian novelists. Ignatius Donnelly's 1890 novel *Caesar's Column* envisions a New York City of 1988 that is illuminated by "the radiance of its millions of magnetic lights, reflected on the sky, like the glare of a great conflagration." It is a place where "night and day are all one." And in *Nineteen Eighty-Four*, George Orwell describes Winston Smith's interrogation room as being brightly lit with no windows. "In this place, he knew instinctively, the lights would never be turned out. It was the place with no darkness." For Orwell, unrelenting illumination is another way to erode individuality and privacy. Indeed, the horror at the center of many of these dystopian futures is the destruction of the individual and the standardization of human beings and their experiences. Whether the future is a communist or capitalist nightmare, the underlying threat of homogeneity is the same.

In the young Soviet Union of the 1920s, lightbulbs were known as "Lenin's lamps," and the national electrification project became linked with a socialist ideological vision. Illuminating a path to a glorious Soviet future, electrification would conquer the threats of capitalism, theology, superstition, social hierarchies, and "the coarse backwardness of village life." Lenin famously said, "Communism is Soviet power plus the electrification of the whole country." Modernization and the inexorable march of technological progress advanced on many fronts, under many different banners.

In 1987, when my mother and I visited Saratov, the city where she attended university, we came across a bust of Pavel Yablochkov in a city park. When I asked her who this man was, she told me he had invented the lightbulb. "That was Edison," I corrected her. "Well, in Russia, Yablochkov invented the lightbulb," she informed me. Later, I learned that Yablochkov had invented a type of arc light known as the "Yablochkov candle" in 1876, three years before Edison's invention. Later still, I learned that Edison and Yablochkov are national heroes that stand for a kind of progress. The truth is, many people invented the lightbulb, incrementally, over centuries.

"With the chronic suppression of dreams, the color is slowly bleached from our lives, contributing to depression—waking life devoid of its naturally expansive dreamy context," writes Naiman, arguing that the entertainment industry strives to quell our dream deficit by offering us prepackaged images. "Are we unwittingly engaging the services of professional dreamers to do our dreaming for us?" he asks. Even if the dream were a commodity that could be packaged and sold, it would be a poor substitute for a real dream, which is the manifestation of an individual's hopes and fears. The dream is an expression of individuality. This is not work that can be outsourced. The consultants can't be called in. Capitalism cannot sell us our dreams, even though, as Crary notes, "there is a broad remodeling of the dream into something like media software or a kind of 'content' to which, in principle, there could be instrumental access."

I recoil at the word *content.* That *content creator* is an actual job makes me despair. Why do we need content? What emptiness are we filling? Are our lives so impoverished that we must swallow more and more content consisting of empty images and vapid slogans? It's like the vanishing caloric density of Cheetos, which melt in your mouth, making your brain think you aren't consuming any calories, so you stuff yourself and are never satisfied. The internet is full of content with vanishing caloric density on which we gorge ourselves, while the world around us burgeons with true content, and so do we. In our dreams, our minds are not creating inane content that can be recorded or commodified; rather, they are doing the ongoing work of the self in its constant becoming.

Three years after Beston lamented our collective loss of darkness in *The Outermost House,* Edison died at the age of eighty-four. "Thomas A. Edison, who made the night brighter for humanity, will be buried in Orange, N.J., today, and as a mark of sorrow at his passing, the nation, at President Hoover's request, will plunge itself into momentary darkness at 10 o'clock tonight," *The New York Times* reported on October 21, 1931.

President Hoover explained the significance of this tribute: "This demonstration of the dependence of the country upon electrical current for its life and health is in itself a monument to Mr. Edison's genius." Indeed, the fact that turning off the lights—rather than the magic of illumination—had become the more dramatic act represented the triumph of light over darkness. We gasp not at artificial light, but at its absence.

Edison's old camping buddies, Henry Ford and Harvey Firestone, attended his funeral. According to *The New York Times*, Mina Edison, his widow, could see from his grave site the skyglow over Manhattan from "the lights his genius gave to the world just fifty-two years ago." Ford sadly reminisced on Edison's last finished work before his death: a piece of rubber that was vulcanized from the juices extracted from goldenrod. He worked until the very end.

VI. Madness

When July Fourth dawns with thunder rumbling and a fine rain falling, we decide to tour the Quincy Mine, an old copper mine. On the seventy-mile drive, the rain falls in terrific sheets, deafening us as it pounds against the metal hull of our car. The mine is crowded, the tour similar to others we have been on. This is all part of my daytime life, with the exception of one moment when the guide turns out the lights and plunges us into utter darkness—presenting the dark as a novelty or gimmick—a requisite of every mine or cave tour I've ever been on. But always a child squawks, or someone gasps or mutters something inane, and the moment quickly becomes unbearable, and then the guide turns back on the lights, banishing darkness before we've truly known it.

On the drive back, the rain becomes a deluge, rendering our windshield wipers useless against the crush of water. Cars creep along with their hazard lights flashing, while some pull over on the shoulder to wait out the storm. We make it back to the parking area near our cabin, then set out on the quarter-mile walk home, discovering a new six-foot-wide stream cutting across our trail. The forest is saturated, glistening, mushroom-scented, turgid, strewn with branches and debris. All night, the engorged river outside our cabin roars.

By the following day, Lake Superior has turned a turbid brown, and all along the shoreline great snarls of wrecked trees and mottled, water-sculpted crags of wood are strewn, churned up and regurgitated by the violence of the storm. Beachcombers wander the shore looking for treasures, marveling at these artifacts of the deep. We stop at the visitor center, where the rangers are busy fielding questions from bewildered tourists. *Why is the lake brown? Is it always brown? How long will it be brown?* The rangers patiently explain that the storm, which dumped more than two inches in just a few hours, roiled up the waters, agitating all the mud and debris. It could be days before the lake is back to its usual self.

That night, in the aftermath of the churning, my aunt Susan comes to me.

Susan, the younger and only sister of my father, spent her entire adult life institutionalized. Every weekend, my grandmother would bring her home to visit for a day. Susan strode frenetically through the rooms of the house, swinging her arm in a wild arc, a cigarette clenched tightly between her fingers, speaking in a low voice that grew alternately agitated, guttural, hysterical, demonic. She changed her clothes compulsively, a dozen times or more in one visit, casting off the old garments in heaps on the bed. Sometimes, she was aware of the people around her—she'd ask my grandmother where a blouse was, she'd tell me what colors to make Minnie Mouse's dress in my coloring book, she'd comment on a movie playing on the TV—but much of the time, she was in the grip of the voices that filled her head as she jabbered deep-throated incantations that sometimes sounded like the Gregorian chants my father listened to on his record player. Susan was in thrall to her own powerful visions.

The Susan I knew was the medicated, stabilized, best-case-scenario version of herself. Before I was born, when she experienced her first visions, she was out of control. By the time I knew her, she was relatively tractable, somewhat sociable. She was also in constant motion. She couldn't sit still long enough to color a picture or watch a TV show. She could barely get through a song on the radio. She didn't drive, read books, cook, sew, work, or any of the things the adults in my world did. She flitted in and out of rooms, always on the move, her mind copiously agitated, buzzing. She had the busiest mind of anyone I knew; she was so busy being Susan that it occupied all of her faculties. Being Susan was the most consuming job in the world.

When Susan comes to me in the Porkies, she appears in a version of a dream that I have been having my whole life. In the original dream, I am with my grandmother and my younger sister and brother, and we have come to Susan's facility to pick her up for a weekend visit, but rather than waiting for her in the bland reception area, we have somehow become imprisoned behind the door where the mentally ill live. In my dreamworld, it's a dark dungeon, vast and cavernous, not a building at all but an underground geologic formation—the inside of a cave or a volcano—and it's my job to lead my grandmother and siblings out to safety. The dream always ended the same way. I was leading my family members single file over a narrow beam that spanned a moat in which horrible monsters roiled and churned while crazy people's voices screamed and jabbered all around us, echoing off the rock, and then someone would fall in and be devoured: my sister or my brother, sometimes my grandmother. In every iteration of the dream, I turn to look back, only to discover I have lost someone to the darkness.

I stopped having the dream when my siblings got older, and then when my own children were very small, it returned. It was exactly the same story, except now I was leading my children through the lair of madness, and my grandmother was rarely with us. In some versions of the dream, the identities of those I was protecting kept metamorphosing; I would be leading my children, but the next time I looked back, they had transformed into my siblings, and then they went back to being my children. It didn't matter who they were, because I felt equally responsible in either case, and I always lost one of them in the end. I kept having the dream for several years, and then, after Susan died in 2016, I stopped having it.

In the Porkies, it returns. I am leading two children in my care through great peril and darkness—only now, we are no longer in a subterranean space. Now, we are creeping through a deep, dark wood, unholy and menacing, surrounded on all sides by unspeakable danger.

"In dreams we see ourselves naked and acting out our real characters," writes Henry David Thoreau. "Our truest life is when we are in dreams awake." Naiman makes a similar point when he writes, "In many respects, dreams are just like waking except much more so." Waking in the middle of the night in the cabin, I mine my dreams for meaning, searching my visions for some essential truth that is not apparent to my waking self. "Often, persons emerged from their first sleep to ponder a kaleidoscope of partially crystalized images, slightly blurred but otherwise vivid tableaus born of their dreams," writes Ekirch. He was writing of preindustrial people who experienced segmented sleep, but he could have been writing about me in the Porkies.

"The widely held truism that all dreaming is the scrambled disguised expression of a repressed wish is a colossal reduction of the multiplicity of dream experiences," Crary writes. "The readiness of much of Western culture to accept the general outlines of such a thesis is merely evidence of the thoroughness with which the primacy of individual desire and want had penetrated and shaped bourgeois self-understandings by the early twentieth century." Dreams, Crary insists, have "trans-individualistic significance"—or they used to—and they offer us the means to "exceed the isolating and privatizing confines of the self." Ironically, it is in our private, inexpressible dream states that we may become most attuned to shared visions for humankind. Our most intensely private dreams can be conduits to a more capacious Dream—in Martin Luther King Jr.'s sense of a vision. That we've muted that channel, or at least turned down its volume, represents a great loss. We do need our dreams, just as we need our poets, our visionaries.

Walt Whitman is well known for his attempts at creating an inclusive vision of the nation, roving over the geography of the country, capturing its places and people in exhaustive catalogs, exuding optimism and bluster in his manspreading lines that fill all the space and break over, seeping to the horizon and beyond. When he famously declares, "I celebrate myself," at the beginning of his groundbreaking 1855 *Leaves of Grass,* he is speaking not only for himself but for an entire nation. He is celebrating all of us, and his enthusiasm for his task is inexhaustible; indeed, his rewriting and reenvisioning of his book became a lifelong project that ended only with his death in 1892. Some scholars view Whitman as a mystic or a prophet, expressing a uniquely American democratic vision wherein the self is positioned at the center of a zeitgeist that breaks down self–other demarcations and merges the individual with the kosmos (his spelling). Indeed, some speculate that it was a mystical experience that led Whitman to create a work as strange and visionary as *Leaves of Grass* in the first place.

Now, though, I think not of Whitman's swaggering daytime self but of his night-writings. In his democratic vision, night as well as day and the sleeping as well as the awake are deserving subjects, and, as he writes in his preface, "the deep between the setting and rising sun" is worthy of poetic treatment. I turn my attention to the fourth poem in the 1855 edition, which over the years went by several titles, including "I wander all night in my vision" (taken from its first line), "Night Poem," and "Sleep-Chasings," until it ultimately came to be known as "The Sleepers" in 1871 and subsequent editions. This poem has always baffled and troubled me.

When I taught this poem in a class on Whitman in early 2020, a month before the pandemic closed our college campus, I insisted it was his second most important poem, after "Song of Myself." I told my students that the critic Paul Zweig saw "The Sleepers" as "the dark twin of 'Song of Myself.'" But my class notes from that day exhibit my uncertainty, my lack of footing in the poem. My analytical mind cannot get a purchase in its amorphousness. *Is the poem about observing sleepers or is the speaker a sleeper? Loss of boundaries between self and others? A plunge into other regions of consciousness? Descent into darkness, ambiguity, madness? Even more fragmented than usual because of the fragmented nature of a nocturnal narrative (which is not a narrative at all)?*

"It is a challenge daunting to the poet's craft: how to make the dream mode of consciousness, the negation and antithesis of wakeful awareness, accessible as conscious experience," writes critic Alan Trachtenberg. "The Sleepers" throws us into a confusing and murky dreamworld that seems to lack logic: We get images of sleepers—including the victims of violence and trauma, the alienated and estranged, as well as happily married couples, sisters, a mother and child—that adhere to Whitman's democratic vision and his penchant for cataloging the breadth of American life, but we also get disjointed narratives about a shipwreck, a swimmer, a slave, a Native American woman, George Washington, Lucifer, and even a whale. At some points, the speaker of the poem seems to be an outside observer watching the action, while at others he seems to merge with those he has been watching, their consciousnesses becoming one. "I dream in my dream all the dreams of the other dreamers," he writes. "And I become the other dreamers." And sleeping, for Whitman, is a democratic, equalizing state. The sleepers "are averaged now. . . . One is no better than the other," he writes. "I swear they are all beautiful, / Every one that sleeps is beautiful. . . . Every thing in the dim night is beautiful."

The porous nature of dream life, coupled with Whitman's vision of a self that is part of a greater whole, a kosmos, means that the poem eludes interpretation, which, after all, is conducted by our analytical minds, our daytime selves. Trachtenberg claims the poem, "dark and obscure as night itself," posits a challenge: "Its parts disconnected, its aura hallucinogenic, the poem tasks the reader to question whether it hangs together and, if so, by what overarching theme or logic." That Whitman dreams the dreams of others and, in fact, *becomes* those other dreamers, risking the dissolution of his self, I would argue, is an act that achieves Crary's vision for building community and greater purpose in dream states. Whitman does, in fact, "exceed the isolating and privatizing confines of the self" in his magnificent dream vision, his dreams becoming a Dream.

One night, my dreams offer me a new vision: I am no longer leading children through the forest; rather, we are following someone, a shadowy, elusive figure who's leading us to safety, if only we can keep up. As I keep glimpsing the person flitting through the trees, I struggle to recognize them. Finally, after what feels like hours of pursuit, I discern the familiar wild swing of the arm: We are following Susan. She is leading us to safety, though she seems unaware that we're even there. Never looking back, she moves rapidly through the forest, and now I see that every time she reappears from behind a tree, she's wearing a different outfit. And even though she's walking and we're running, we're never able to close the distance between us. I wonder how Susan can be leading us to safety, when to me she'd always represented the danger of insanity. Suddenly, it occurs to me that she is saving us not from the madness of madness, but from the madness of those who try to control the madness. All her life, she lived under the care of people who tried to harness her visions, to temper them, to return her to the banal, blanched world the rest of us inhabit—and now, finally, she is roving free of them through my nighttime forest. What if the true madness is not in her but in the rest of the world, the inexorable machine of progress that puts its stamp of uniformity on all of us, and leaches out of us the original and the strange? Many saints were possessed with gripping visions, and I suspect if they lived in our world now, they would have been judged mad instead of holy.

I never saw Susan sleeping. I can't even imagine her asleep. She had boundless energy; until she was over sixty and using a walker, I never saw her sit still for more than a few minutes at a time. On one rare Christmas Eve when she spent the night at my grandparents' house, I heard her moving around, pacing up and down the upstairs hallway. I even met her there in the middle of the night as she strode through the dark with a glowing cigarette pinched between her fingers, jabbering about mistletoe and jockeys. Wearing a long, old-fashioned nightgown, she was like an apparition unloosed from a fictional world, a ghostly somnambulist from a milieu that made no sense—a gothic horror novel about a madwoman imprisoned in an attic, but set in a dreamscape too personally symbolic to convey any meaning—and she was too bent on her task to see me at all. A small child hiding in the shadows, I slunk past her on my way to the bathroom. She was a true creature of the night, her night self indistinguishable from her day self, her powerful visions governing her life always, night and day.

"Were it not for the fact that we are asleep when they occur, we would be obliged to say that our dreams are formally psychotic and that we are all, during dreaming, formally delirious and demented," writes sleep researcher Allan Hobson. “The study of dreams is the study of a model of mental illness.” Many people have drawn the comparison between dreaming and madness. Charles Dickens, in an essay titled “Night Walks,” wonders about the inhabitants of a hospital for the insane that he passes on his late-night rambles. “Are not the sane and the insane equal at night as the sane lie a dreaming? Are not all of us outside this hospital, who dream, more or less in the condition of those inside it, every night of our lives?” he writes. “I wonder that the great master who knew everything, when he called Sleep the death of each day’s life, did not call Dreams the insanity of each day’s sanity.”

Indeed, it might be our fear of what appears to be madness that makes us reject and suppress our dreams. As Christopher Dewdney writes in *Acquainted with the Night: Excursions Through the World After Dark*, “It is a subconscious awareness of our own instability, our potential for madness, that underscores our nocturnal insecurities.” Encountering our night selves might mean acknowledging our unstable, unhinged, even insane, selves.

“By the nature of their illness, paranoid schizophrenics have a very rich, if out of control, hallucinatory inner life,” writes Naiman. “Hallucinations, which can be understood as an intrusion of dreamlike experiences into waking consciousness, may represent the polar opposite of dream suppression—a kind of dream expulsion.”

Perhaps Susan was dreaming always. And what she glimpsed of what the rest of us call the waking world was always through the murky scrim of her powerful visions.

When I was a young child, sometimes I sat very still, intently listening, waiting for the voices inside my head to start speaking to me, waiting to be wrenched from reality by a hallucination so potent that I would become a stranger to everyone around me. I waited in anticipation and terror to be possessed by my singular vision, but it never happened.

As I follow Susan through my Porkies dreamworld, though, I understand it is no longer her kind of madness that I fear. Rather than a warning of what might happen to me, or to any of us, she becomes a beacon of resistance, insisting on her own way of being in a world that prizes conformity. I understand, moving through the shadowy world between wakefulness and sleep, that we have been gripped with what perhaps can be called a different sort of collective madness: We exist more and more in virtual spaces accessed via screens where we create our digital surrogates, form and maintain relationships, erect worlds and enact lives separate from the temporally and geographically bound forms of our corporeal bodies. We are distilling ourselves to carefully curated digital stand-ins.

Crary suggests that this urge to disappear ourselves from the limitations of our bodily existence is linked directly to fears of impending climate catastrophe. "The more one identifies with the insubstantial electronic surrogates for the physical self, the more one seems to conjure an exemption from the biocide underway everywhere on the planet," he writes. "At the same time, one becomes chillingly oblivious to the fragility and transience of actual living things." Perhaps this is why I feel a desperate need, a compulsion, to go to dark and remote places, to bring along my children and to drag them out of the tent in the middle of the night and show them the Milky Way, to insist they see the beautiful wild—in all its dimensions—before it's gone. Perhaps this is why I mine my dreams for some version of myself that exists outside of a world broken by greed and consumerism, outside of the vapid digital realms where we cower and post images in despair.

Darkness has become an outpost of wilderness. Sleeping and dreaming have been demoted to the category of banal bodily functions. We have made it possible to glut on all that was in short supply during most of humankind's history—sugar, fat, light—but have not learned to moderate our cravings. We have been reduced to pure consumers, to content devourers, to gluttons who cannot get enough. Perhaps our most radical turn away from the wild is in becoming an organism severed from others, awash in toxic manufactured goods, staring at screens that give us an impoverished simulacrum of the luminous, breathing world. We have banished all for the sake of a blue light that promises to cater to our personal proclivities but does little more than offer standardized images that never satiate our deepest hunger. We are flattened, pixelated in the process, losing something of what it means to be a human being. We become, in Forster's words, flat characters to one another and even to ourselves. When we work so hard at *making memories*—another term that makes me cringe—are we just barking our existence into the vast chamber of the internet as our lives slip away between our fingers? We seem to believe that our vapid posts, substantiated by curated photos, can preserve these moments, as though the internet has become our main repository for memory, as though meaning can be manufactured and content can fill us up, satiate our spiritual hunger.

I listen to my son sleeping in the cabin, hoping and fearing for his future. At least in sleep, he is protected. At least in sleep, especially in this dark, dark place, he is beyond the reach of the dangers of the lit world. He is, I hope, caught up in dreams, roaming his own inner wilderness.

VII. Dreamers

I suspect that Nikola Tesla, the mysterious genius of the age of electricity, was much more a man of the darkness than Edison. Throughout his life, he was gripped by powerful visions, intuiting much of what Edison came to know through trial and error. After Edison died, Tesla told *The New York Times*,

> His method was inefficient in the extreme, for an immense ground had to be covered to get anything at all unless blind chance intervened and, at first, I was almost a sorry witness of his doings, knowing that just a little theory and calculation would have saved him 90 per cent of his labor. But he had a veritable contempt for book learning and mathematical knowledge, trusting himself entirely to his inventor's instinct and practical American sense.

It is that same practical American sense that values blind determination and doggedness, that holds up the blustering, blundering anti-intellectualism of the self-made man hellbent on progress, that insists on positivity and brightness, that shuns darkness, poetry, the intuitive, the mystical.

As an old man, Tesla recounted a story about his beloved childhood cat, Macak. "In the dusk of the evening, as I stroked Macak's back, I saw a miracle that made me speechless with amazement. Macak's back was a sheet of light and my hand produced a shower of sparks loud enough to be heard all over the house." Tesla's father told him, "This is nothing but electricity, the same thing you see through the trees in a storm." His mother said, "Stop playing with this cat. He might start a fire." But young Tesla was mesmerized, and he wondered, "Is nature a gigantic cat? If so, who strokes its back? It can only be God, I concluded."

But there was more. "It was getting darker, and soon the candles were lighted. Macak took a few steps through the room. He shook his paws as though he were treading on wet ground. I looked at him attentively. Did I see something or was it an illusion? I strained my eyes and perceived distinctly that his body was surrounded by a halo like the aureola of a saint!"

This moment stayed with Tesla his entire life. "I cannot exaggerate the effect of this marvelous night on my childish imagination.

Day after day I have asked myself 'what is electricity?' and found no answer. Eighty years have gone by since that time and I still ask the same question, unable to answer it."

I go back to the opening line of Whitman's poem: "I wander all night in my vision." I linger on the word *vision.* To have a vision is radically different from seeing an image. Among the definitions for *vision* are the following: *something seen in a dream, trance, or ecstasy; a thought, concept, or object formed by the imagination; the act or power of imagination; unusual discernment or foresight.* An *image,* on the other hand, is *a visual representation of something, such as a likeness of an object produced on a photographic material or a picture produced on an electronic display.* It is also *a mental conception held in common by members of a group and symbolic of a basic attitude and orientation; a popular conception (as of a person, institution, or nation) projected especially through the mass media; exact likeness.* We are bombarded by images, which require no act of imagination and lead us inexorably toward standardization. It is vision that we need.

In grad school I spent three years immersed in the language of Whitman, transcribing and encoding digital copies of his manuscripts for a major digital humanities project, The Walt Whitman Archive. I imagined how easily Whitman—who had spent decades of his life revising and rewriting his book in six distinct editions—could have refashioned himself on the internet, as he blogged, and later, tweeted, his song of America. I thought of our work—making every known word he'd ever written available to anyone with an internet connection—as a continuation of his work, and I imagined how satisfied he would be to have all his corpus widely available on the web. What could be more democratic?

But now, I'm not so sure. Now, as I think of the many hours I spent poring over images of his manuscripts on oversized monitors magnified to 300 percent, I wonder what he'd make of all of us staring so intently at screens, as though our lives depended on it. I've never held a Whitman manuscript in my hand, never traced the indentations of his pencil, never touched paper that he touched. The internet made such touch obsolete. And we insisted it didn't matter—that the image was enough, that the transcription was enough. But is it? "This is no book, / Who touches this, touches a man," Whitman writes in "So Long!" a closing poem he added to his 1860 edition. He remains the embodied, fleshly poet to the end, and while I had always read these lines to mean a joining of minds, perhaps the physical heft of the book is equally important. The consummate bookmaker, Whitman insists on the primacy of the material artifact. The ether is not enough for him; haunting the web would never satisfy him. "It is I you hold, and who holds you, / I spring from the pages into your arms," he insists, calling himself into physical presence, his words nearly becoming flesh.

During the pandemic, when we all sheltered in place, I kept on my desk two copies of Whitman. One was an 1860 edition of *Leaves of Grass*, a gift from my husband, and the only edition I own from Whitman's lifetime. The other was my mother's Russian translation from her grad school days, Kornei Chukovsky's 1966 *My Whitman*, which she brought to the United States and held onto long after she had abandoned her career as an academic in the Soviet Union. I would pick up the books and leaf through them, or sometimes just hold them, as I thought of my students, who had gone home for spring break and never returned. The remainder of my Whitman class happened online. My students sat in their homes across the country, reading writers responding to Whitman: those who over the course of a century and a half have written back to him, argued with him, reimagined his poetic project. The latter portion of the class was devoted entirely to the dreamers who followed in his wake.

"Not a single moment, old beautiful Walt Whitman, / have I stopped seeing your beard full of butterflies," writes Federico García Lorca. "What thoughts I have of you tonight, Walt Whitman, for I walked down the sidestreets under the trees with a headache self-conscious looking at the full moon," adds Allen Ginsberg. "I touched a hand and it was / the hand of Walt Whitman," says Pablo Neruda. "Walt Whitman is wearing mirrored sunglasses / behind the wheel / of the buttercup yellow Mercury, / so that only when I see him do I see me," offers Gillian Conoley. These voices filled the spring of the pandemic, as we sat far apart reading. "Whitman's wild children still sleeping there, / Awake and walk in the open air," writes Lawrence Ferlinghetti. "Don't touch me, Walt, I'm a sparrow on a live wire, / it may be death to step from ourselves and connect," advises Chou Ping. "How impossible to have a reasonable relation / with the self no matter what you say, Walt Whitman," says Dean Young. "I too am a descendant of Walt Whitman," declares June Jordan.

For their final assignment, my students remade Whitman for themselves, writing poems and stories and letters, creating collages and paintings, then photographing and scanning their work to share it with me, so I could peer at their dreams on my screen. One student, Dalanie Beach, looked to Whitman for a way through the pandemic, asking,

> To what degree can
> we maintain control
> of the atoms
> we borrow
> from the grass?

In an accompanying piece of visual art, Dalanie created a canvas out of a tree cookie with the bark still attached, embellished it with glued-on bone, shell, and stone, then painted Whitman's bearded visage as a ghostly image, as though his face naturally emerged there in the heartwood of a sawn tree. The work, Dalanie explained, was inspired by their Grandpa Bill. "Whitman and my Grandpa Bill share a vision of the natural world, seeing it as a vast orchestra of interrelated cycles, patterns, and rhythms," they wrote. "I imagine that Whitman and my Grandpa Bill—two men with thoughtful, yet talkative souls, who seek refuge in Nature, in Being and Seeing, and of loving and knowing one is loved—would get along very well."

Though Tesla required little sleep, often getting by on just three hours, he was a man prone to powerful visions. When he was twenty-four and living in Budapest, he and a friend took a walk one day in the city park and recited poetry. Tesla knew much poetry by heart, including Goethe's *Faust*. The setting sun reminded him of a passage, which he then recited. As he was saying the words of the poem, he recounted years later, "the idea came like a flash of lightning and in an instant the truth was revealed. I drew with a stick on the sand the diagram shown six years later in my address before the American Institute of Electrical Engineers." He had just invented the induction motor.

A dozen years later, having returned to Croatia to visit his ailing mother, he had a vision in his sleep, seeing "a cloud carrying angelic figures of marvelous beauty, one of whom gazed upon me lovingly and gradually assumed the features of my mother. The vision slowly floated across the room and vanished, and I was awakened by an indescribably sweet song of many voices. In that instant a certainty, which no words can express, came upon me that my mother had just died. And it was true."

He also foresaw the technology of our present. "When wireless is perfectly applied . . . we shall be able to communicate with one another instantly, irrespective of distance," he said. "Not only this, but through television and telephone we shall see and hear one another as perfectly as though we were face to face, despite intervening distances of thousands of miles; and the instruments through which we shall be able to do this will be amazingly simple compared with our present telephone. A man will be able to carry one in his vest pocket." Tesla also described getting the daily newspaper "wirelessly" and an automobile that could "perform a great variety of operations with something akin to judgment."

And his vision extended beyond the technology to the kind of world he hoped it would create. One of Tesla's biographers, Richard Munson, writes of the inventor's "principled belief that technology should transcend the marketplace and that invention should not just be tied to profits. He aimed high, perhaps higher than any other inventor. He worked tirelessly to offer electric power freely to the world, to build automatons that would reduce life's drudgery, and to provide machines that could abolish war."

Tesla died in 1943 at the age of eighty-six. A true dreamer, he was a scientist with the soul of a poet.

Our contemporary society has pushed dreamers—visionaries—to the peripheries. "The imaginative capability of the dreaming sleeper underwent a relentless erosion, and the vitiated identity of a visionary was left over for a tolerated minority of poets, artists, and mad people," writes Crary. "Modernization could not proceed in a world populated with large numbers of individuals who believed in the value or potency of their own internal visions or voices."

Rather than listening to dreamers, we often call them mad. This is a phenomenon that Rachel Aviv explores in *Strangers to Ourselves: Unsettled Minds and the Stories That Make Us,* in which she relates the story of a woman named Bapu who was a Hindu mystic and poet in Chennai, southern India. When she was diagnosed with schizophrenia by a doctor educated in the Western tradition, she felt that her own story about herself as a mystic had been "forcibly replaced by a new one about mental illness," which was "clumsily out of step with her self-conception" and made her feel "devalued." Perhaps it should come as no surprise that studies conducted by the World Health Organization have found that "people were more likely to recover from schizophrenia in developing nations than in developed ones." Despite our American cult of individualism, we offer a narrow range of standardized options in regard to mental health.

Even those of us who are not suffering an acute mental health crisis are likely to feel the pressure of a culture that values standardization and abounds with light-filled metaphors: We should look at the bright side, see the light, lighten up, and so forth. The ceaseless messages that any dark mood should be lightened, bleached by drugs or a change in attitude, are part of a mindset that has been dubbed "toxic positivity." Some of us, as philosopher Mariana Alessandri tells us, are dark by nature, and we are right to feel sad and depressed and anxious. "I have always felt emotionally dark," she writes. "I'm an angry person genetically, and I feel sad most of the time." She continues, "The Light Metaphor relentlessly insists that darkness is ugly, negative, miserable." Her book *Night Vision* is a defense of dark moods. "In the light, our dark moods make us look broken," she writes. "In the dark, though, we look fully human."

And to be fully human is to experience the full range of emotional states.

Instead, we pathologize unpleasant emotions, leading to overmedication and estrangement from our true selves. "Mental health has become synonymous with the absence of symptoms, rather than with a return to a person's baseline, her mood or personality before and between periods of crisis," Aviv writes. And some people, having been medicated for most of their lives, don't even know what their baseline is. Rather than banishing or masking unpleasant states—sadness, inadequacy, loneliness, anxiety, discomfort, fear—I have tried to embrace the range of experiences that means I'm alive. Rather than standardizing emotions to a narrow range, I have lived my life in the frightening, murky depths. "With all our lights we push away our fear, and by pushing away our fear, we are a little less alive," writes Bogard.

VIII. Darkness

My sojourn in darkness comes to an end on our penultimate day in the Porkies. I awake, leaving behind my aunts in the forest, not knowing that I will not see them again, that my connection to darkness is about to break. During a brief stop at the visitor center in the afternoon, I turn on my phone, and discover a flurry of voicemails: my older child D., away at a Chinese immersion camp at a remote ski resort in Minnesota, has COVID. The news wrenches me back to the waking world. I immediately call, text, and email my husband. I try to reach the camp. I get through to no one. Eventually, we have to leave the Wi-Fi of the visitor center and return to our cabin.

We start packing and cleaning. I periodically wander out of the cabin with my phone and meander up and down the trails, seeking a cell connection, scanning the horizon for a ridge, a place of hope. The trees have become obstacles, my remoteness a nuisance. Finally, in a clearing on a rise, I get through to my husband: D. has been placed in an isolation cabin with other COVID patients and is being cared for by a Chinese doctor who is nursing them back to health with cucumber water. Next, I reach D., who is indecisive and discouraged. They want me to drive east tomorrow to rescue them, but they also don't want to risk getting me and their brother sick during the long car ride home.

It is deep twilight before I return to the cabin. The boy is already asleep. That final night, I keep my phone close to me, turned on, even though I have no cell service. Suddenly wrenched back into the illuminated world, I dip in and out of shallow dreams about my malfunctioning devices. Several times, I take my phone outside to the rise where I had previously found a pocket of connectivity, and I gaze intently at its glowing face, looking for news. I am utterly blind to the darkness around me. I have already left that world.

In the morning, D. sends a message: They will stick it out in the COVID cabin, where they are maintaining their language immersion pledge, still speaking Mandarin, learning the words for symptoms and medications. The boy and I clear out of the cabin and start driving home.

I have been writing this essay for eighteen months. I have read twenty-seven books about darkness and night and sleeping and dreaming. This project began at the crest of summer and is ending at the trough of winter, when the days are dark. Or perhaps I should invert my thinking: In winter I stand at the crest of darkness, in summer the trough. And yet I light up the winter darkness with artificial light, spending too much time staring at the blue glare of a screen. Facebook is awash in hopeful messages about the solstice, about the return of light. Friends post Christmas greetings and New Year's resolutions or, alternatively, screeds against New Year's resolutions. One offers personal saints for the New Year, their names drawn out of a pretzel jar.

One post, about *Merriam-Webster*'s 2023 word of the year, catches my eye: *Authentic*, meaning "not false or imitation" or "true to one's own personality, spirit, or character." The article points out, "Ironically, with 'authentic content creators' now recognized as the gold standard for building trust, 'authenticity' has become a performance." In other words, authenticity is no longer authentic. In typical wild-goose-chase fashion, I keep seeking, trying to find something reassuring. The Dictionary.com word of the year is *hallucinate*, in the sense of artificial intelligence: "to produce false information contrary to the intent of the user and present it as if true and factual." This word, repurposed for our current moment, is also telling. Our anxieties about being authentic may also be tied up with the fact that we must now distinguish ourselves from robots, somehow tell ourselves apart from deep fakes. None of this is reassuring.

Then I see a post from my former student Dalanie, who writes with the news that Grandpa Bill "went through the door to discover the secrets of the universe." They add, "I am grateful to have been by his side, holding his hand as he set out on this new adventure." *I bequeath myself to the dirt to grow from the grass I love, / If you want me again look for me under your bootsoles*, I immediately think, and I consider writing this, or invoking Whitman in some way, but I am loath to write anything of substance on an impoverished digital medium that indiscriminately offers up wrenching heartbreak among humorous cat videos and products that promise steel abs, each post carrying the same visual weight, so I write nothing.

I turn away from the screen, turn out the lights. I sit in the orange-gray haze of city darkness, and I think about how one of my colleagues, in talking to his first-year writing students about AI, tells them there's a difference between a machine's language and theirs: A machine has only language—grammar, syntax, vocabulary mined from millions of sources—but no referents. But they—they have the entire world. "Don't outsource your mind," he tells them. "Our writing has to touch the world."

The night before we leave the Porkies, I open up the logbook to the first empty page. It's my turn to offer some words about my experience, to speak to the artists who will follow me. But my thoughts are scattered—mentally, I have already left—and I attempt to say too much, creating a fragmented listicle of tips rather than a meaningful sustained meditation. "Relish the darkness," I write in one of my bullet points. "The rest of our lives has too much illumination." It feels like the easy wisdom of a social media post. I am creating content.

Perhaps my aunts came to me in the Porkies in part because they never led online lives, never did the enervating work of erecting digital personas, stretching themselves across platforms, reducing their experiences to standardized emojis or hashtags, desperately shoring up selves made of ones and zeros, empty calories, fireworks and misdirection, blue glare and existential despair. In my final dream of them, I no longer have any children in my care; I am alone in the dark woods, pursuing both Olga and Susan, who move in their own special ways through the sinuous darkness. Olga runs in the nude like a graceful animal, while Susan strides purposefully, swinging her arm, magically changing her clothes as she goes. They do not seem aware of one another or of me, but they move in the same direction, at the same speed, and I follow them, breathless, falling farther and farther behind, until they disappear into the deepest, most impenetrable heartwood of the night.

"There is a well-known critical tradition, going back to the late nineteenth century, which identifies the standardization of experience as one of the defining attributes of Western modernity," writes Crary. Susan's and Olga's lives burgeoned beyond standardized experience. They were probably the most authentic people I've known, and I don't use that term lightly. In seeking them in the darkness, in chasing them through my Porkies dreamworld, perhaps I was doing the long, protracted work of mourning them. I missed Olga, especially the many years she was gone from my life, due to geographical distance. I saw her last in 1999. And I missed Susan, not just as I knew her but also as she had once been. We lose people in different ways.

My only two aunts by blood, the younger and only sisters of my parents, were born and lived their entire lives and died in one place—yet in their minds they roved farther than anyone else I have known. In life, they never stepped foot in my hemlock forest, but I leave them there now. I leave them to the darkness, where they await me, where I will one day join them.

In memory of

Susan Bea Renfro
July 29, 1947–January 19, 2016
Riverside, California

Olga Alexandrovna Stulova
April 26, 1958–July 23, 2020
Samara, Russia

Interlude ONE THANKSGIVING IN MAINE

One Thanksgiving in Maine, when the adults are having third glasses of wine and loosening their belts and the kids have slogged back inside, red-faced and snow-dazed, the mother, midsentence, glances at the girls now whipping the cream for pies, and realizes that her boy, the youngest, has not returned. She is saying to someone that she now understands Robert Frost, after all these years, but she stops and turns to the window, seeing the gloaming, the unyielding cold, the wide yard that slopes away to a treed, blue-tinged landscape. When the kids went out the light was steady white, their colorful parkas bright spots on snow, but now the scene is shifted, ominous, and as she moves to the window to look for her boy, she asks her daughter, "Where's your brother?" The girl comes to the window and they both spot him, lying in the snow on his side, immobile, and from here they can't make out anything but his utter stillness. And the girl turns to her mother with wide eyes, taking responsibility for this calamity—whatever it is—for leaving behind her little brother, only six. And the mother holds her breath, watching for movement, calculating how long he's been alone, rebuking herself for taking that extra glass of wine that made her lose track of time and children. But really, hasn't it been only ten minutes—fifteen?—since the last of the other children came traipsing inside? The girl raises her knuckles to rap on the glass.

But there is another perspective: the boy, outside, alone. The other children, a gaggle of girls—sister, cousins—have left him. And perhaps this is his first plunge into aloneness: that profound feeling of being singular in a wide, cold world. What is it to be pressed between the sky and the snow, held here by the thumb of gravity? What is this hush of a snowy landscape, this stillness? How long can he remain here, alone, unnoticed? And why is he alone? And what is being alone?

Back inside, the girl's knuckles strike glass, and immediately the boy jolts up, alert, and looks at the house. And the mother feels foolish, for fearing the worst. A boy does not lie down in snow and go to sleep forever in ten minutes. Or half an hour. A boy has more sense. He comes inside when he is cold. He has legs to carry him. And the girl, who too has been holding her breath, exhales. "He wasn't asleep," she says. "He was just lying there." Then she pulls open the sliding glass door and calls, "Come inside!"

And the boy? The boy hears the sharp rap, severing his tie to snow and cold. He sits up and looks at the pooling yellow light with the faces floating there contained like fish in an aquarium. He is outside in the still wide world, and those faces are held captive by glass and light and warmth. His sister calls; he stands, trudges back, not toward reunion but toward a further cleaving from stillness and aloneness and perhaps even himself. There is his warm cloying mother and sister whose faces float in incandescence, and here is the blue gleam of snow, and it is this other colder touch that he craves.

And even right after all this happens, already it seems a long time ago. The mother's mind has worried at the event, abrading it on all sides like sand over jagged glass, until it is polished, the sharp contours worn away. She has scoured it until *one Thanksgiving in Maine* becomes the only possible beginning to this story, granting it the patina of timelessness. And it appeals to her because every Thanksgiving of her childhood happened three thousand miles away in California, where snow and Maine both seemed an impossibility. And this is why she never understood Robert Frost and why she mistrusts the cold and why seeing a child lying in the snow can make her heart seize.

So she takes the story for herself, appropriating all parts of it, insisting on its timelessness. Because mothers stand at windows looking out at children who are there, or who are not there. Because mothers stand at windows and see things that make their hearts seize. Because mothers stand at windows and watch their children leave them, in a thousand different ways. They leave and they leave and they leave until they do not come back. This is the kind of ballooning the mother's mind demands: making a story mean everything. Looking at a boy in snow and thinking of all mothers and all children everywhere, at all times.

And because the mother has sucked the thing smooth and thin, like a lozenge, because just a sliver and the flavor remains, she wants the boy's story. Weeks later, months later, she asks him. What were you doing out there? What were you thinking about? Why? Why?

"It was cold," he says. "It was just cold."

This does not appease his mother, so he says, "I was just lying there thinking about building the biggest snowman ever."

"But you weren't building the snowman," she presses.

"The snow was too icy. You need fresh, sticky snow. That snow was old with ice frozen on the top."

"Didn't it feel cold?"

"Yeah."

"How cold?"

"As cold as snow with ice on top of it. That cold."

His mother seems disappointed, or at least not sated, so he thinks. And then he says, "I was listening to the snow."

His mother leans forward. "And what did you hear?"

"It was like it was talking in a different language, not a language of people but a language all its own."

And then the daughter speaks, because the daughter loves stories as much as the mother, and she wants to be part of this story. "I came inside to help put whipped cream on pies—and then we called him in together."

The boy looks at his mother, hoping this is enough. He has a mother who plucks moments of his life—ensnaring them—her mind as relentless as a viewfinder. His mother is a camera freezing life, rendering it motionless. So sometimes he says the things he thinks she wants to hear—*I was listening to the snow*—which then overwrite the truth, whatever the truth is. Sometimes there is no truth. That's the truth. But that is not enough for his mother, who is demanding always of stories, smothering him with her need, like the press of a too hot hand, like the wall of heat in the aquarium of the house where all those captive faces float.

Maybe the bite of the blank snow on skin is having no story at all. Maybe the snow just is. Maybe the stillness of a winter landscape is the world saying *Just hush for a moment. Hush. There is no story. Hush.*

Isle Royale National Park

THE BONE SEEKERS

Isle Royale National Park, Michigan
June 2024

"Shed!" Pattie called.

The five of us, creeping through the forest, came to a halt. As our leader Jeff made his way over to Pattie, I took the opportunity to rest, leaning on my walking stick, watching Pattie hold up the moose antler she'd found and Jeff measure the diameter of its base where it had been attached to the pedicle. While he recorded the measurement and GPS coordinates in a small all-weather notebook, Pattie sawed an X in the base of the antler to mark it as recorded, then laid it back down where she'd found it.

We started moving again, walking in a picket line loosely spread out, canvassing the forest floor. Part of a Moosewatch Expedition team of volunteers ranging in age from mid-teens to mid-sixties, we were on Isle Royale—the island national park in the northwest corner of Lake Superior—to look for moose bones.

Just a couple of days into our weeklong expedition, I had already gotten separated—briefly—from the group during our first picket line because my full concentration was on making my next move, navigating over fallen trees and through swamps, as we spent eight-hour days inching our way through the boreal understory. What had I gotten myself into? I periodically looked over at my sixteen-year-old son Nick, who seemed to have no trouble staying with the others or navigating his way through a maze of downed trees. He was even finding sheds and bones.

I had yet to find anything in the dense vegetation of the forest; in fact, searching for moose bones came in a distant fourth on my list of priorities, after paying attention to my footing, keeping track of the rest of the group, and battling mosquitoes and black flies. I kept taking my head net off and putting it back on. It obscured my vision, but without it, I was driven mad by insects.

"Bone!" Dave yelled.

I gratefully stumbled toward him, eager for a break. We all converged around the femur he'd found. Nick took off his daypack to retrieve our kill kit and removed from it a bright orange flag that he hung in a tree above the bone to mark its location.

Then, we all fanned out in different directions, looking for other bones, which might have been dragged by wolves up to a couple hundred yards. I tried to think like a wolf: If I were making off with pieces of a moose carcass, which way would I go? Studying the topography of the site, I wandered uphill and then down, pushing aside foliage in the hope of glimpsing the white wink of bone. Instead, I was lured by the flashes of birch bark all over the forest floor. We searched for half an hour, but finding no additional bones, we left the femur where it lay and moved on.

Back in camp, as we were finishing dinner, Jeff asked me if I was enjoying the expedition.

"I will enjoy it in retrospect," I told him. "Right now, it's difficult and uncomfortable. But that's not how I'll remember it."

"That," Jeff said, "is the definition of Type II fun."

Isle Royale National Park, an archipelago of one large island of just over 200 square miles surrounded by 450 smaller islands, is known for being one of the least visited and one of the most revisited national parks. Around 20,000 people make it to the island each year; by comparison, Yellowstone can draw more visitors in a single summer day. Part of the challenge of visiting Isle Royale is simply getting there: boat or seaplane are the only modes of transportation. The journey from the mainland takes up to six hours. This is why so few make it to the island. But upon visiting once, people are inclined to return, year after year.

This was our third trip—and our most difficult. Nick and I first spent seventeen days on the island when I served as artist-in-residence in 2021. The following year, we backpacked the forty miles across the island, from Windigo to Rock Harbor, sometimes covering a dozen miles a day. Visitors are drawn back to the park by the beauty and ferocity of Lake Superior, the rugged wilderness character of the island, the stunning vistas, as well as the opportunities for hiking, backpacking, kayaking, canoeing, fishing, viewing the night sky, and appreciating wildlife—including moose and wolves. This time, we had come for the moose—dead ones.

In addition to all that Isle Royale offers recreational visitors, the island also offers a "natural laboratory" for scientists. Since 1958 it has been the site of the wolf-moose project, the longest running predator-prey study in the world. And since 1988, the project has relied on volunteers—about sixty per summer—to comb portions of the island looking for moose bones. More than a thousand volunteers have come to Isle Royale to search for bones in the past three and a half decades. When Nick and I first heard about the project two years ago, we were intrigued and vowed to sign up when he turned sixteen—the minimum age to participate. The trip would give us another way to know the island we had grown to love.

As volunteers for the 2024 Moosewatch Team III, we set out in early June from Copper Harbor via the *Isle Royale Queen IV*. Landing in the rain at Rock Harbor, the eighteen of us were ferried to Bangsund Cabin—the summer headquarters of the study since 1960—where Rolf and Candy Peterson distributed supplies and marching orders. Split up into four teams of four to five people each, we were being dispatched to different parts of the island. Candy kept rhubarb bars and cinnamon bread coming out of the oven as she ran through gear lists with volunteers while Rolf pored over maps with team leaders. The Petersons have been spending summers in Bangsund, a century-old fishing cabin, since 1970; Rolf has dedicated his entire career to the project, and Candy has been his partner every step of the way.

Rolf gave Jeff four known targets for our group to locate: two with GPS coordinates, two with location descriptions. We were to begin our trek at Daisy Farm and then head northeast, eventually going along the Greenstone Ridge toward the easternmost part of the island.

"Bone!"

We were looking for one of the targets for which we had a description only: The moose was purportedly located off the Mount

Franklin Trail, after the trail junction, southwest of the north end of the long boardwalk. And here it was—or at least here was part of it, a leg bone with the hoof still attached, lying in a bog.

The others immediately went to work: finding the best way across the swamp to reach the bone, fanning out into the adjacent area to look for the other parts. I followed behind, reluctant about the prospect of walking through a swamp or handling a dead moose that looked relatively fresh.

On higher ground, perhaps twenty yards away, we found another leg, and then the skull still attached to the vertebrae—the kill site. After photographing the bones in situ, we began collecting them in one area, sorting them and counting them, looking for arthritis and other pathologies. Jeff recorded information on a small card: the GPS coordinates, the vegetation and terrain, the age and sex of the moose, the date and cause of death, the distance the bones were scattered, the number of each type of bone. The moose, Jeff told us, had been killed by wolves, probably early this year. A Moosewatch volunteer since 2002 and the senior member of our group, Jeff had experience at numerous kill sites, and in his other life, when he wasn't leading teams looking for dead moose, he was a self-described data programming guy, so keeping track of information came naturally to him.

We collected the bones that are most useful to researchers: the skull, mandibles, incisors, and metatarsus. The cementum rings in the roots of incisors can be counted to determine the age of the moose, and the metatarsus provides information about prenatal health (and the health of the mother) as well as the animal's first year of life.

But the bones still had clots of flesh on them, and we needed to sever the skull from the vertebrae. I fetched the bone saw and a plastic bag from the kill kit, and then Pattie jumped in to do the hard work, sawing and twisting the skull until it finally came detached from the vertebrae. I watched with a mix of fascination and revulsion. Pattie was in her early fifties, just a couple of years older than me; her day job was working as an electrician building transmissions, but she also had training as a nurse, and her knowledge of anatomy was evident as she sorted bones. Even though this was her first Moosewatch, she seized every opportunity to be involved. I looked at her with admiration. She was someone who worked with her hands, who directly manipulated the world, while I was largely an observer. I was used to hanging back, watching, composing a story.

As the others tied up the bones we'd collected with parachute cord into a package we dubbed the "stinky suitcase," I vowed to get past my reservations about touching dead flesh. I had imagined finding gleaming, dry skeletons lying just a short distance from a trail, in open, sunny glades; instead, we were fighting our way through soggy, bug-ridden, overgrown terrain to hunt down slimy, smelly bones that we had to violently sunder into pieces. And then we had to carry them for miles. I had clearly not taken to heart the warnings on the wolf-moose project's website describing the Moosewatch program: "Unlike most backpacking trips, these expeditions often end with packs that are considerably heavier than they were at the beginning, because of all the moose bones collected. From a single adult moose skeleton, Moosewatchers may pack up to 15 pounds of bones." I had read all of this, but the warnings had seemed abstract until I was actually hoisting up a putrid mass of bones and flesh. But every new find taught me something. Soon, I hoped, I would feel competent at a kill site, knowing exactly what to do—and doing it.

That night in the tent, as I listened to the loons calling to each other in Tobin Harbor, I thought about the moose we had found, about his final stand before his death, about the wolves that ended his life in order to nourish their own. I remembered a passage from *Restoring the Balance,* a recent book by one of the leaders of the wolf-moose project, John A. Vucetich, in which he imagines a moose's life-ending confrontation with wolves: "Teeth, swinging hooves, bloody snow, spinning sky, faintness, a once proud and still massive shoulder hitting the ground hard, tearing of flesh, fading, and then nothing."

A wolf's life is no less fraught with danger. Attacking prey ten times their size, wolves are often injured and even killed by the powerful kicks of moose. Researchers have found that wolves prey on weak, vulnerable moose—the young, the old, the sick, the injured, the malnourished—that are easier to take down. A healthy moose does not run from wolves but instead stands its ground or even charges its attackers. Vulnerable moose, on the other hand, run from danger, a behavior that prompts wolves to chase and attack the animal. The majority of wolf-moose interactions end after just a few seconds of the wolves "testing" a moose: "moose commonly stand and pugnaciously face the wolves, which take the cue and leave," writes Rolf in his book, *The Wolves of Isle Royale*. Moose are "tested" in this way many times over the course of their lives. Durward Allen, the first lead researcher on the project, referred to these encounters as the moose's "annual physical," which they keep passing—until they don't.

Necropsies of island wolves have found many to be riddled with healed breaks and other injuries from a lifetime of violent encounters with moose and with members of their own species. Indeed, much of what we now know about wolves has come from Isle Royale. According to the wolf-moose project website, the study "began during the darkest hours for wolves in North America—humans had driven wolves to extinction in large portions of their former range." What researchers learned on Isle Royale, beginning in 1958, helped to change public attitudes about wolves—and continues to shape our thinking as the study leads to new insights.

The project has also amassed a great deal of data on moose. The collection of moose bones from more than five thousand moose that have died on the island since the 1950s is a veritable museum, preserving specimens for future scientists to ask questions that we can't even dream of now. The bones contain data that we haven't yet learned to read—but what we have learned has far-reaching implications.

Moose teeth, in addition to revealing the animal's age, have also revealed trends in air pollution. Researchers have noted that the levels of radioactive carbon in the teeth reflect nuclear weapons testing conducted during the Cold War. Some of the records go back even earlier—Adolph Murie collected three large cabinets full of moose bones from the island during his time there in 1929 and 1930. Rolf writes, "Moose, unknowingly acting as biological time capsules, had stored in their teeth a record of large-scale ecological change."

He also notes, "Isle Royale still provides the best information available on patterns of natural mortality for moose in the absence of the gun."

The bone collection has allowed researchers to develop profiles for entire populations of animals, leading to many new findings, some of which have direct applications to human health. On average, 40 percent of Isle Royale moose that live to the age of ten develop arthritis, but those born during severe winters are much more likely to develop the disease than those born during plentiful winters, suggesting there's a connection between poor nutrition early in life and arthritis in adulthood. Another study that investigated links among three bone diseases that affect humans and moose—periodontitis, osteoporosis, and osteoarthritis—found that moose with periodontitis were much more likely to have severe forms of osteoarthritis and osteoporosis. These studies have ramifications for the treatment and prevention of bone diseases in humans.

Having read books, articles, and the study's recent annual reports, I knew all of this prior to coming on the Moosewatch trip. I had pored over descriptions of the winter study, when Rolf and other researchers fly in a small plane over the island, observing the wolves and conducting the annual moose census. Most years the winter study lasts around six weeks, but in early 2024 the study was cut severely short, running for just two weeks, due to a warm winter; a lack of ice in Washington Harbor meant the plane had nowhere to land. Still, the study lasted long enough to allow researchers to conduct the annual wolf and moose census. As of early 2024, there were 30 wolves and 840 moose on the island.

I had read about the population fluctuations over the years. The moose population rose as high as 2,400 before plummeting to 400 in the mid-nineties, and the wolf population topped out at 50 in 1980 before eventually dropping to just 2 animals in 2016. The population dynamics are much more complex than researchers first thought. A web of factors—including the widespread effects of climate change—has contributed to these fluctuations. Due in part to the effects of inbreeding and the spread of parvovirus from dogs in the early 1980s, the wolf population was all but wiped out until the

National Park Service made the controversial move to reintroduce wolves to the island in 2018 and 2019. Though some of the nineteen relocated wolves died and at least one returned to the mainland, the remaining wolves have established themselves and reproduced, maintaining a predator presence on the island.

According to the project website, "the focused purpose of the Isle Royale wolf-moose project has been to predict and understand a relatively simple natural system. But the more we studied, the more we came to realize how poor our previous explanations had been." The remarkable longevity of the study has allowed scientists to come to epistemological conclusions, not just scientific ones. "Natural history might be much like human history—explainable, but not predictable," the site notes. "If we see Nature as a system whose future we can predict, then we will be confident in our efforts to control and manage Nature. If, in Nature, we are more impressed by its essentially contingent, and hence unpredictable character, then our relationship will be more strongly rooted in striving to live within the boundaries of Nature's beautifully dynamic variation." All of which leads scientists to a humanist place: humility. As Rolf writes in his book, "Science simply illuminates in a modest way that which invigorates the human soul." Our national parks, he writes, are "both laboratories and cathedrals." I had previously revered the national parks primarily as cathedrals; this trip was my chance to know one of them as a laboratory. And I wanted more than book knowledge. I wanted to move beyond passive receptacle of knowledge to participant.

Each day is more trying and exhausting than the last, I wrote in my notebook, reflecting on the previous day's long slog to our new campsite just off the Duncan-Tobin portage trail. We had hiked seven miles in heavy rain with full packs. Nick's raincoat had proved inadequate, and he was drenched to the waist and chilled when we arrived. With the rain still coming down, no one was eager to start unpacking and setting up camp. Nick sat miserably on the ground, and then his nose started bleeding. *That was the low point of yesterday,* I wrote. Jeff and Dave set to work: They put up a tarp in a low stand of trees, started water boiling for hot chocolate, and got Nick under the shelter with a bandanna to stanch the blood. I dug out a dry shirt and coat from his pack and got him out of his wet clothes.

Fortunes can change quickly in the wilderness. Just a couple of hours later, after the rain had subsided, after we'd set up the tent, Nick was hanging his socks to dry on some trees along the ridge when he looked down into the gulch behind our campsite and said in a low voice, "Mom, I see a wolf!"

I was perhaps fifteen feet away, sorting gear, and I immediately looked in the direction he was facing, but except for a rustling in the trees, I detected nothing. And then the wolf was gone.

When we told the others about the sighting, they marveled at Nick's luck. Wolves are notoriously shy around humans. To see a living moose on Isle Royale is common, but to see a wolf is rare indeed.

I was writing all of this in the tent in the early morning—but I heard the others up, drinking coffee, preparing for another day, so I finally joined them. Today, we'd be canvassing the forest in a picket line—a.k.a. aimlessly wandering, hoping to stumble upon a dead moose.

Later, I would write it all down: donning wet socks and wet boots for the third day in a row, creeping through the forest at a pace of under a mile an hour, diverting around the toppled trees and burned snags of the virtually impenetrable Horne Fire area that burned in 2021, climbing over and ducking under countless obstacles. We found a number of sheds and several moose. *I have so many bug bites my collar was red with blood when I took my shirt off*, I would write later. *I found an antler by stepping on it—I am clearly not the most observant person.*

"Bone!" Dave was standing over what appeared to be a mossy rock, but when he lifted it, I saw it for what it was: an old moose skull. Dave could see bones when they looked nothing like bones. In his early fifties, he was on his eleventh Moosewatch and had developed the ability to see moose bones when they were mere moss-covered suggestions embedded in the forest floor.

Nearby, we found the other bones, all of them close together. "This moose starved," Jeff told us, adding that it likely perished in the moose die-off of 1996. Rather than being dragged apart by wolves, scavengers—foxes and ravens—had shifted the bones short distances, leaving them in a small area, relatively easy to find. What we couldn't locate were the incisors. Pattie and I searched for them in the area where we found the mandibles. I remembered what I'd read in the moose bone diagrams we'd been sent before the trip: "Incisors can 'burrow' into the ground up to 6 inches below the mandibles." We went down farther than six inches but found only roots and rocks. Still, we had the skull, the mandibles, and the metatarsus—which was enough. And I much preferred the old and mossy moose to the fresh and slimy ones. I even volunteered to carry this one.

Over dinner, we talked about the expedition. "Is it harder than you thought it would be?" Jeff wanted to know.

"Yes." Nick and I answered almost at the same time.

"How so?"

I started to say something about how hard it was to go off trail for entire days, how my five-mile-a-day treadmill routine had not prepared me for clambering over endless obstacles, how terrible the bugs were, how miserably wet my feet were, but it wasn't any one of those things—it was all of them.

"It's not as physically hard as it's psychologically hard," Nick said. And he was right.

Then we talked about how the rain, the damp, the unknown difficulties that lay ahead were more mentally taxing than the actual physical challenges of our exertions. In the end, though, we agreed that we would all be glad we had done it. We were back to Type II fun.

Type II fun, a term commonly used in pop psychology and by outdoor enthusiasts, refers to activities that are enjoyable not as they are occurring but in retrospect. "These types of fun are often associated with pursuits of endurance like sports or outdoor activities (e.g., mountaineering, hiking, etc.), where the pleasure is derived from overcoming adversity, reflecting on the experience, and the sense of achievement it brings," writes Mike Rucker for *Psychology Today.*

Mountain climbers in particular have embraced the term; it appears in Matt Samet's *Climbing Dictionary,* which traces its origin to Rainer Newberry, a geology professor in Alaska who invented the Fun Scale while teaching a field geology class in 1985. Since that time, the concept has been embraced by people engaging in a wide array of activities—including those looking for dead moose.

In an article for *Outside Magazine,* Amanda Loudin makes a connection between Type II fun and a 2017 study in the *Journal for Consumer Research,* "Selling Pain to the Saturated Self," that investigates the phenomenon of people paying for painful experiences like the Tough Mudder, an adventure challenge of twenty-five difficult (and often painful) military-style obstacles. The study's authors argue that "the reduced physicality of office life and the intense boredom contemporary work practices seem to generate" coupled with "the demands of sustaining a coherent yet constantly revised biographical narrative" lead to a "saturated self." They add, "The weariness of being a self is something knowledge workers seem especially keen to escape." This is especially true for the "cognitariat," those "knowledge workers who are not only working jobs of limited physicality but also feel the burden of constant self-actualization." Painful experiences, the researchers write, help the cognitariat to momentarily escape themselves, though "they eventually go back to the unrelenting construction of self-identity that characterizes modernity."

All of this sounds eerily familiar; in my other life, I spend most of my working hours writing at a computer or teaching in a classroom. In my writing life, I am once removed from my experiences, but in my teaching life, I sometimes feel twice removed, teaching others how to write about their experiences. What's more, maintaining a teaching persona feels like an extreme, performative version of "the unrelenting construction of self-identity." I have plenty of reasons to seek temporary escapes from my real life. Still, I cannot accept the simplistic conclusion that I am seeking pain in order to escape myself—or at least that can't be the full explanation.

Another way of getting at the appeal of Type II fun is to examine the limitations of Type I fun. Many—dare I say most?—tourists are after Type I fun, and while there's something to be said for feeling good in the moment, these easy experiences often don't require reflection, the kind of processing that brings out the multidimensionality of more challenging experiences. Traditional tourism tends to provide Type I fun, which at its worst can turn the tourist into a mere spectator and consumer. "To be a mass tourist, for me, is to become a pure late-date American: alien, ignorant, greedy for something you cannot ever have, disappointed in a way you can never admit," writes David Foster Wallace in an article on the Maine Lobster Festival, a tourist venue focused on eating—which is nearly always Type I fun. He continues:

> It is to spoil, by way of sheer ontology, the very unspoiledness you are there to experience. It is to impose yourself on places that in all noneconomic ways would be better, realer, without you. It is, in lines and gridlock and transaction after transaction, to confront a dimension of yourself that is as inescapable as it is painful: As a tourist, you become economically significant but existentially loathsome, an insect on a dead thing.

Like Wallace, I am averse to the kind of mass tourism that often feels like gluttony: voyeuristically feasting on scenery, rendering architecture, people, nature as two-dimensional tableaux. The destination becomes a commodity, and we mere consumers of it. Jamaica Kincaid writes, "An ugly thing, that is what you are when you become a tourist, an ugly, empty thing, a stupid thing, a piece of rubbish pausing here and there to gaze at this and taste that." We are less despicable to ourselves when our tourism isn't of the exploitive, consumerist variety. This, I think, explains much of the appeal of ecotourism and various kinds of service trips as well as citizen science projects—including Moosewatch—which enable a traveler to be a participant in a place, someone who contributes, someone with a conscience and a thinking mind.

* * *

We were on our way back to Daisy Farm, moose bones strapped all over our packs and two "stinky suitcases" tied up with cord that we traded off as we hiked. Occasionally we passed people on the trail who gawked at our strange luggage. "Dead moose. We ate well this week," Jeff joked to one day-hiker.

We had found eight moose—the four targets along with four additional moose we'd discovered as we combed the terrain—and now our sojourn in the wilderness was almost at an end. Tomorrow Rolf would be picking us up in the boat to take us and our bone collection back to Bangsund. But first, we had one more moose to go after—an antlered skull that two of Rolf's interns had found and told us about as we crossed paths on the trail.

After setting up camp at Daisy Farm, we set out for our last moose. Finally, with our trip almost at an end, I felt that I had my bearings, and I was eager for the adventure. Maybe it was just that I knew we were nearly finished. Maybe it was that most of the hike was on trail, and we were carrying only daypacks, and when we finally plunged off trail into the forest, the terrain didn't seem nearly as difficult as before. Maybe it was that we had a specific destination set in the GPS, and that Nick was leading the way, and when we finally came upon the moose, it was my storybook moose, the one I had first imagined, the one in a clearing, his clean, blanched bones spread out on a rocky outcropping. Maybe it was that I had learned that the bones had a story to tell, that I had fully internalized the truth of a kill site: This was a place where a creature larger than me, a sentient being, had made his final stand. This was the site of his death, and we had made a pilgrimage to it to learn what we could, to read in his death something about him but also something about ourselves. I knew his bones held stories—some of which we could read right here, others we'd have to wait for. He was an old bull moose that had died of malnutrition, with the smaller antlers typical in bulls over a decade old, but he had surprisingly little arthritis for his age. We would carry some of his bones away with us—Nick cradling his antlered skull in his arms all the way back to camp—and we would pass the bones on to others who would read more stories in them. *It was a beautiful kill site,* I would later write. *Such beautiful bones.*

Moosewatch allowed me to become, for a week, someone I didn't normally get to be: a scientist, an explorer, a person of the outdoors. During the trip, I could imagine I was someone different—someone who knows more than I do, who has greater practical competence and greater confidence in what my body can do, someone who spends more time outdoors than I do and who is at home in the elements, unbothered by wet feet and sore muscles. Coupled with that was an underlying feeling that if I spent enough time there, I would learn something—about myself, about living in the world stripped of most conveniences, encumbrances, the layers of modern life that pad and muffle us, cutting us off from the sharp edge of existence in the wild. I had come here to learn about the world unadorned of human presence (as much as that is possible), to peek into the lives of other species, to decenter myself for a moment (or to try). The scope, the thoughtfulness, and the slowness of the wolf-moose project appealed to me. This was a kind of science that was not about flashy breakthroughs being published at breakneck speed. This was boots-on-the-ground and hours-mired-in-swamps kind of science.

In his book on the North Woods, *What Should a Clever Moose Eat?*, ecologist John Pastor writes of a growing trend among researchers to rely on existing datasets rather than heading out to the field to collect their own data. "Unfortunately," Pastor writes, "with research funds being increasingly difficult to procure and with the increased pressure for young scientists to publish to get a job interview or to obtain tenure, using compilations of data from the literature or online databases becomes an attractive alternative to spending years getting a grant and then working several more years in the field to test hypotheses more rigorously." And science, he argues, is impoverished as a result. Though he doesn't use the term, Pastor seems to be advocating for "slow science," a growing movement among some scientists.

The wolf-moose project, focused on predator-prey dynamics over time, is by necessity slow. Led by just a handful of researchers—first Durward Allen, then Rolf Peterson, and now John Vucetich and Sarah Hoy—with contributions from countless others, it outlives careers and lives, representing a plodding and meandering kind of science, one that requires patience and the long view—which are sorely missing from our world. After working on the project for decades, after being surprised, again and again, by the complexity of the interactions within the Isle Royale ecosystem, Vucetich writes that he started to question the very purpose of science. Perhaps, rather than manipulating nature to get the most out of it, the purpose of science should be attempting "to understand the extent to which nature is complicated beyond hopes for predicting her behavior, as a means of learning to tread more lightly." Science, he suggests, might consist of two kinds of knowledge. "The first kind helps us do things in the world," while the second kind "sets our attitudes to compassion for nature's living things." This second kind of knowledge, he argues, "may be more important," concluding that a central goal of science should be "the advancement of wonderment-generating knowledge." The scope of the wolf-moose project gives researchers the time and ability to ask bigger questions such as these concerning the purpose of science and the nature of human inquiry. It also allows them to do better science, testing explanations and developing new ones. "The danger in paying attention for only a short while is developing a strong sense for an erroneous idea," Vucetich writes. "What we accrete best are disproven ideas. Somehow, if not ironically, it brings us closer to some truth."

When I lived in Connecticut, I spent nine years watching a white oak grow from an acorn to a tree, measuring it and counting its leaves, and the only reason I stopped was that I moved away and the tree was too big to take with me. The gradual accumulation of data—a single set of moose bones hauled out of the backcountry—appeals to that in me which desires to be witness to a whole greater than myself, to watch the world not in frenetic soundbites and clips and social media quips but in the sedate pace of natural processes. Just as I want to watch a tree grow, I want to be part of the slow blooming of human knowledge over decades, created by many minds that take the time to really pay attention, nourished by thinkers who honor our capacity for wonder and acknowledge that laboratories and cathedrals both contribute to our understanding of our place in the universe.

Back at Bangsund, a cheerful and mild pandemonium reigned. Rolf ferried the groups back, one by one, while Candy offered chips and salsa, worked on feast preparations, and welcomed the occasional visitors who wandered in on the trail from Edisen Fishery a mile away. Returning Moosewatchers set up their tents all around Bangsund for their final night, exchanged moose tales from the week, and took turns taking wilderness showers—a pail of hot water with a dipper between two tarps. I wandered around the "mooseum of pathology" and looked at the hundreds of moose bones on display—racks of antlered skulls, stacks of mandibles and metatarsi, femurs completely dislocated from hip sockets due to severe arthritis.

Rolf and Candy's attention was pulled in every direction, but still they managed to talk to all the Moosewatchers, attentively listen to our stories, inspect our bone hauls. Our group had found nine moose and twenty-five sheds, covering nearly sixty miles, more than twenty of them off trail. As the other groups came in and hauled their bones out of the boat onto the beach, I admired them—the antlered skulls, the long metatarsi, the stinky packages held together with cord or plastic. In a brief lull, Candy talked to me about her life on the island: raising two children here, living among moose and wolves and learning about death, working as a hospice volunteer. I told her about a literature class I've been teaching for years on the theme of death and dying. We discussed the ways that society obscures death: the health-care industry hiding or medicalizing death, the death-care industry cloaking death in euphemisms and secret rites that are performed outside the view of grieving loved ones. I remembered something I had read in an essay on death by Philip R. Stone: "We no longer hear or perhaps think of people 'dying of mortality.'" Standing there surrounded by the bones of moose, Candy and I talked of Leo Tolstoy and Virginia Woolf, of society's fear of death, of the spiritual dimension of the natural world—and then she went back inside the cabin to chop cabbage.

Later, when Rolf was free, I asked him what he could tell us about our old bull moose. He pointed to the constriction around the pedicles and told me it was a sign of testosterone insufficiency, which indicated the moose was old. How old? Fourteen or fifteen, he guessed, which is old for a male moose on Isle Royale. The oldest known male lived to eighteen (females can live to twenty, and one made it to twenty-two). Our moose's information would be entered into the database, and his teeth would be used to determine his exact age. Then we talked about Russia—an interest we shared in common—since I was born there and Rolf has always wanted to go there for the moose conferences. We talked about another place we had in common—Lincoln, Nebraska—where I had done my PhD and where Rolf had traveled to see the ancient elephant bones in the state museum. As I listened to him, in my mind Russia suddenly teemed with moose, and Nebraska with elephants, becoming places not just of people but of animals.

Then it was time for the feast, so the twenty of us—eighteen volunteers, Rolf, and Candy—sat down at picnic tables for a meal of lasagna, garlic bread, carrots, and cabbage, with brownies and cheesecake for dessert. Teams stood up, one by one, to make their reports. Moosewatchers talked about having wet feet for days, being devoured by insects, seeing living moose, going over beaver dams, dealing with equipment malfunctions. Nick reported on his wolf sighting. Another volunteer told the saga of his boots falling apart. One group described pulling a "floater"—a moose that had died in the water—out of a pond. The evening ended with a singalong.

Way up north on a Royale Isle
A Moosewatch team chose to spend a while
They hiked and climbed and made their search
And learned to tell the difference between bone and birch.

On the boat ride back to the mainland, I read Candy's *A View from the Wolf's Eye*, a book I had neglected to read in my extensive research. Candy's take is much more personal than the other works I'd read. After meeting Rolf her junior year at Wellesley and getting to know him, she writes, "I was certain that I would follow this Scandinavian nature-lover anywhere. It was satisfying for me, an unfocused generalist, to support Rolf, so well suited to his chosen field of wildlife research. Rolf's dream was novel and large enough for two people." That dream has remained capacious enough to sustain a partnership of more than fifty years. "Rolf seeks to understand the physical world," she writes. "I am fascinated by our spiritual existence." Her lessons from the island are more personal but no less essential. Reading her words, I felt like I was still talking to her, extending the conversation that we'd never quite finished.

"Completely engaged in the present and not aspiring to live forever, wild animals seem content, unencumbered by guilt about the past, envy about the present, or worry about the future. The whole system is without malice," she writes, and continues:

> We, unaware and/or uncertain of our role in nature, are whiners and worrywarts, forever devising methods to avoid hardship, alleviate pain, and prolong life, cursing bad fortune, ungrateful for blessings. Unwilling to confront death's inevitability and our constant vulnerability, we invest in security measures that can actually increase our fears. Our culture of materialism and control enslaves us and robs us of our faith and our sense of well-being; I am careful whom I call a "dumb animal."

Periodically, when I took a break from the book, Nick and I talked about what we would do the next time we came to the island—because already we knew there would be a next time. *I already want to come back,* I wrote in my notebook. *I already miss it.* Coming out of the wilderness was always like this, relief and regret swirling together, my experience metamorphosing into story, difficulty rewritten as accomplishment. And part of the story, I realized, was about my own tired, aging body that I kept taking on treks, challenging it to stay fit. On the cusp of fifty, I saw that every trip into the wilderness was now an act of resistance to my own senescence. One day, my old bones will have their own story to tell.

As I looked out at the vast waters of Lake Superior, I couldn't believe I was leaving. My body was on the boat, but my mind remained on the island, moving through the forests and swamps, looking for moose bones, trying to glean what the moose and wolves could teach me about living and dying. I thought about the old bull moose in the clearing, his final moments there, his collapse. I thought of him falling and never rising. Later, we would tell stories about our adventure—severing skulls from vertebrae, assembling stinky suitcases, hiking into the backcountry and hauling out dead moose—but that is only a small part of what happened. What else happened was this: The fallen moose have become a part of me. I carry them with me, and they mean something, but their lessons are not quickly or easily extracted. Maybe it's just that animals live the one life they are given to their utmost, and then they die. As Candy writes, "perhaps moose simply know when it is time to die"—whether they're brought down by wolves or starvation. They die of mortality, their deaths unobscured, unadorned, straightforward and blatant as white bones gleaming on a ridge.

CODA
Out of the Current

Samara, Russia
July 1999

Sitting on a Volga beach, you think of time in terms of rocks, how every landscape bears layers of time, like geologic strata, with fine demarcations between seasons, sudden rifts marking cataclysmic events. But while matter leaves behind traces, time deposits no visible sediment: the tepid sand beneath you, the hazy sunshine, the singsong voices of children—the ineluctable now obstructs all other times.

You watch passing ships—long low barges, cruise ships like gleaming white cities, tiny droning motorboats that leave frenetic waves in their wake. You look over the placid lines of the beach: the wet sand where land meets water, the glint of smoke-blue river like a wide steel blade slicing the land from the sky, the narrow dark strip of island near the horizon. People doze or peel hard-boiled eggs or deal hands of Durak with sandy cards, but your eyes are drawn to a woman teaching her five-year-old daughter to swim near shore. These are your people. The girl splashes, laughing, while her mother supports her with a firm hand, giving instructions in a low voice. Though you were born in a hospital not far from here, you're twenty-four now and an American, and this is the first you've been back in nearly a decade. The last time, this was still Kuybyshev, a "closed" city with a defense industry, and your grandparents, still living, were eking out their final years on rationed Soviet food. Looking at the river, you are now and not-now just as you are home and not-home.

All of this before you seems evanescent, a picture imposed on thin fabric that might flutter aside, allowing you to glimpse the other layers accrued here. You might see a crew of nineteenth-century burlaks, yoked together, moving like a single crippled insect up the riverbank, against the current, towing a barge like a monstrous hunk of driftwood, leaning into their effort as though walking into a gale, their doggedly canted poses suggesting that even at rest they will lean, that even in deepest sleep they will perpetually strain against an invisible burden.

Down the shore, a fisherman wades into the river to his thighs and stands, his pole extended, and watching his timeless pose you feel it might be daybreak in autumn in another year altogether—1943, perhaps—and the mute fisherman is the only witness in the frigid dawn when the official state ship arrives, Stalin on deck grimly looking to shore. In a history that didn't come to pass, Moscow has fallen to the Germans, and Stalin has retreated to his second capital, Kuybyshev, positioned on this easternmost point of the Volga where it makes an abrupt turn, the Samara Bend, around the Zhiguli Mountains. Though the war is long past and Stalin is long dead, his bunker remains, thirty-seven meters underground, complete with artwork on the walls and parquet floors. He never did retreat here in wartime, but last week you toured his bunker, helping the interpreter with translations; "world-shaking," she said to the puzzled American couple on your tour, and you clarified: "earthquake." As the fisherman begins to reel in his catch, you see that the gleaming reel's motion is smooth and modern, that it's a relic of the present.

You look back to your people: The woman has taken the girl out deeper, and she is coaxing her to float on her back, to trust the water—and abruptly it is 1984, and your mother, who married an American and has been gone six years, has returned for the summer with her three children, two of them—your younger sister and brother—American-born. To escape the oppressive heat of your grandparents' apartment, you head for the Volga, baffling the female KGB agent keeping tabs on your mother and her entourage of American kids and Russian relatives. The agent is forced to slip away and hastily purchase a swimsuit so that she doesn't look conspicuous on the beach and so that your mother and you and everyone else can go on pretending that you don't know you're being followed. But you hardly notice the agent bulging out of her too-small Soviet swimsuit; you just head for the water, and what you remember most about that summer is learning to swim, being held aloft in the water by adult hands, and later, by the Volga herself.

You rise and enter the water. The girl comes to you and wraps herself around you. She is your cousin, but she calls you her sister, because a cousin and a sister are not so far apart in Russian, and because she lives with just her mother and craves family. As she encircles you in her limbs and says your name, you understand that you are sisters because your mothers are sisters and because you both were born here in the Samara Bend of the Volga River. You turn to watch her mother swim out to the buoys. "That's my mama," the girl says in Russian, pointing at the river. You hold onto your cousin, who is your sister, who seems nearly to be yourself, and what you want most is to crumble time as easily as mineral gives way under a rock hammer, to excavate this landscape in the temporal dimension, to see yourself for what you are—an organism buoyed by the waters of the Volga, trapped in matter and time, your life having hardly begun and simultaneously already spent, a fossil.

Isle Royale National Park

ACKNOWLEDGMENTS

I am grateful to the publications in which essays of this book first appeared.

A version of "The Twentieth Bear" appeared in *Terrain.org*, December 19, 2019. Portions also appeared in "The View Through the Crack" in *Creative Nonfiction*, no. 61 (Fall 2016), and *Places Journal*, October 2016.

"Panorama of a Life" appeared in *South Dakota Review* 56, no. 1 (Fall 2021).

"Betula" appeared in the anthology *Two Countries: U.S. Daughters and Sons of Immigrant Parents: An Anthology of Flash Memoir, Personal Essays, and Poetry*, edited by Tina Schumann, Red Hen Press, 2017.

"The Season of Birds and Stones" appeared in *Alaska Quarterly Review* 41, no. 3 & 4 (Summer & Fall 2025).

"Birds I've Known" appeared in *Short Reads*, no. 049 (February 28, 2024).

"Loon Boy," which was named the winner in creative nonfiction in *Terrain.org*'s 13th Annual Contest, appeared in *Terrain.org*, March 3, 2023.

A longer version of "Island Life, with Boy" appeared in the National Park Service Isle Royale Artist-in-Residence Gallery for 2021.

"Moving: A Triptych" appeared in *Flyway: Journal of Writing and Environment*, Winter/Spring 2024.

A version of "The Night Follows Close" appeared in *River Styx*, Spring 2025.

"One Thanksgiving in Maine" appeared in *The Fourth River*, no. 16 (2019), and was reprinted in *Short Reads*, no. 088 (November 27, 2024).

A version of "Out of the Current" appeared in *Orion Magazine*, July/August 2013.

I am grateful to all the park rangers, park staff, volunteers, and stewards of our public lands I have encountered on my travels, and to all those who have ventured outside with me: Jonathan Shafer, Bob and Tina King, Cass Ray, Jay Elhard, Ali Barnes, Emily Lester, Greg Henry, Dan Irelan, Sherrie McCabe, Katie Urban, Tom and Kendra Gale, Ellie Connolly, Christopher Amidon, Katie Keller, Mariah Reading, Jeremy Caro-Delvaille and his daughters Germaine, Marisa, and Jeanine, James Engelhardt, Jeff Holden, Pattie Evans, David Beck, Rolf and Candy Peterson, Denali bus drivers Mike, Mona, Elton, and Erland, the countless other rangers and volunteers whose names I have forgotten or never learned, and also my brother Alex. Last but not least, I am grateful to my first hiking companion, my uncle Ray; though we have not spoken in many years, I will always cherish our long-ago treks in the mountains and orange groves and wild beautiful places of my Southern California childhood.

Thank you to those who have helped me shape these stories and who championed them: Erin Striff, Melanie Pappadis Faranello, Aimee LaBrie, Clara Rae Marie Bosak-Schroeder, Elizabeth Dodd, Simmons Buntin, Lee Ann Roripaugh, Hattie Fletcher, Debra Marquart, Claire Walla, Ronald Spatz, Tina Schumann, and also the countless other editors who worked quietly behind the scenes on the wonderful publications that first published these essays. And a special thank you to D., who had the vision for this final iteration of this collection. I am grateful also to Nicole Walker, Sarah Shermyen, and the entire team at the University of Georgia Press who have made this book a reality.

Thank you also to my wonderful students at Saint Mary's College—and especially to those in my Whitman course in spring of 2020 and my nature and environmental writing courses in spring of 2021 and spring of 2023—who inspire me to keep reading and writing. Thank you, Dalanie Beach, for allowing me to quote from your work. I also owe a debt of gratitude to the students I taught at Westfield State University, 2012–19, who helped me become a teacher of writing.

Also, thank you to Virge Kask, scientific illustrator at the University of Connecticut, for her wonderful workshop on scientific illustration (which I took twice!), and to the James L. Goodwin Conservation Center Master Naturalist Program in Hampton, Connecticut, where I learned a great deal, even if I was far from a stellar student and never did attain master naturalist status. Thank you to the National Park Service and Michigan Department of Natural Resources for their support of writers and artists through their artist-in-residence programs, and to Saint Mary's College for providing travel funds to allow me to take advantage of residencies.

Last but not least, thank you to my parents, Paul and Irina Renfro, who have supported my writing all along, and my husband Doug, who remains ever unperturbed and equanimous when I abruptly announce I absolutely must go live in the woods for the better part of a month. And thank you to my kids, who have patiently and (mostly) cheerfully accompanied me on countless adventures and who so often become the unwitting characters in the story of my life.

SOURCES

Alessandri, Mariana. *Night Vision: Seeing Ourselves Through Dark Moods*. Princeton University Press, 2023.

Aviv, Rachel. *Strangers to Ourselves: Unsettled Minds and the Stories That Make Us*. Picador, 2023.

Barnes, Burton Verne. *Michigan Trees: A Guide to the Trees of Michigan and the Great Lakes Region*. University of Michigan Press, 1981.

Berry, Wendell. "To Know the Dark." In *The Selected Poems of Wendell Berry*, 68. Counterpoint, 1999.

Beston, Henry. *The Outermost House*. 1928. Reprint, Holt Paperbacks, 2003.

Bogard, Paul. *The End of Night: Searching for Natural Darkness in an Age of Artificial Light*. Back Bay, 2014.

Bonta, Marcia Myers. "Margaret Morse Nice: Ethologist of the Song Sparrow." In *Women in the Field: America's Pioneering Women Naturalists*, 222–31. Texas A&M University Press, 1991.

Brox, Jane. *Brilliant: The Evolution of Artificial Light*. Mariner, 2011.

Bures, Frank. "There Is Nothing Quite Like the Calls from a Loon. Hollywood Can't Get Enough of Them, Either." *Minnesota Star Tribune*, April 14, 2019.

"Camp in the Remote Backwoods of This Beautiful Island Park." *National Geographic*. Accessed July 20, 2025. https://www.nationalgeographic.com/travel/national-parks/article/isle-royale-national-park.

Chen, Eve. "'Nothing Like It': What Makes Isle Royale Park So Extraordinary." *USA Today*, December 5, 2023.

Crary, Jonathan. *24/7: Late Capitalism and the End of Sleep*. Verso, 2014.

Cronon, William. "The Trouble with Wilderness; or, Getting Back to the Wrong Nature." In *Uncommon Ground: Rethinking the Human Place in Nature*, edited by William Cronon, 69–90. Norton, 1995.

Davis, Cynthia J. *Charlotte Perkins Gilman: A Biography*. Stanford University Press, 2010.

Declaration in Defense of the Night Sky and the Right to Starlight (La Palma Declaration). International Conference in Defense of the Quality of the Night Sky and the Right to Observe the Stars, La Palma, Canary Islands, Spain, 2007.

Demer, Lisa. "Denali Park Hiker's Camera Offers Clues to Bear Attack." *Anchorage Daily News*, August 27, 2021.

Dewdney, Christopher. *Acquainted with the Night: Excursions Through the World After Dark*. Bloomsbury, 2005.

Dickens, Charles. "Night Walks." *The Uncommercial Traveller*. 1905. https://www.gutenberg.org/ebooks/914.

"The Dictionary.com Word of the Year Is *Hallucinate*." Dictionary.com, December 12, 2023.

Donnelly, Ignatius. *Caesar's Column: A Story of the Twentieth Century*. 1890. Reprint, CreateSpace, 2017.

Dowd, Marion, and Robert Hensey, eds. *The Archaeology of Darkness*. Oxbow, 2016.

Duriscoe, Dan. "Preserving Pristine Night Skies in National Parks and the Wilderness Ethic." *George Wright Forum*, 2001.

"Edison Is Buried on 52nd Anniversary of Electric Light." *The New York Times*, October 22, 1931, 1.

Ekirch, A. Roger. *At Day's Close: Night in Times Past*. Norton, 2006.

Finn, Daniel. "The Story of the Grand Collective Project That Launched Yuri Gagarin into Space." *The Wire Science*, April 13, 2021. https://science.thewire.in/society/history/the-story-of-the-grand-collective-project-that-launched-yuri-gagarin-into-space/.

Forster, E. M. *Aspects of the Novel*. 1927. Reprint, Mariner, 1956.

Freeberg, Ernest. *The Age of Edison: Electric Light and the Invention of Modern America*. Penguin, 2013.

Gilman, Charlotte Perkins. *Herland*. 1915. Reprint, Dover, 1998.

———. *The Living of Charlotte Perkins Gilman*. 1935. Reprint, University of Wisconsin Press, 1991.

———. *The Yellow Wall-Paper and Other Stories*. Oxford University Press, 1996.

Gottschall, Jonathan. *The Storytelling Animal: How Stories Make Us Human*. Mariner, 2013.

Grigoriadis, Vanessa. "A Death of One's Own." *New York Magazine*, November 30, 2003.

Grobstein, Paul. "Revisiting Science in Culture: Science as Story Telling and Story Revising." *Journal of Research Practice* 1, no. 1 (2005).

Heilbrun, Carolyn G. *Writing a Woman's Life*. 1988. Reprint, Norton, 2008.

Hobson, J. Allan. *The Dreaming Brain: How the Brain Creates Both the Sense and the Nonsense of Dreams*. Basic, 1988.

Hoy, Sarah R., Rolf O. Peterson, and John Vucetich. *Ecological Studies of Wolves on Isle Royale: Annual Report, 2023–2024*. College of Forest Resources and Environmental Science, Michigan Technological University, Houghton, 2024.

Huxley, Aldous. *Brave New World*. 1932. Reprint, Harper Perennial, 1989.

Jabr, Ferris. "What the Supercool Arctic Ground Squirrel Teaches Us About the Brain's Resilience." *Scientific American*, June 26, 2012.

Julian-Fralish, Christopher J., Stacey L. Julian-Fralish, and James S. Fralish. *The Porcupine Wilderness Journals*. Stacis, 2001.

Kimmerer, Robin Wall. *Braiding Sweetgrass: Indigenous Wisdom, Scientific Knowledge, and the Teachings of Plants*. Milkweed Editions, 2013.

Kincaid, Jamaica. "A Small Place." In *Touchstone Anthology of Contemporary Creative Nonfiction: Work from 1970 to Present*, edited by Lex Williford and Michael Martone, 257–64. Touchstone, 2007.

Kyff, Rob. "Loons, Moons and Loony Toons." Creators Syndicate, July 28, 2021. https://www.creators.com/read/rob-kyff-word-guy/07/21/loons-moons-and-loony-toons.

Laursen, Eric. "Lenin's Lamps." *Wonders & Marvels* (blog), February 2, 2013. http://www.wondersandmarvels.com/2013/02/lenins-lamps.html.

Lopez, Barry. "Landscape and Narrative." In *Crossing Open Ground*, 61–71. Knopf Doubleday, 1989.

Loudin, Amanda. "Why Type-Two Fun Feels So Good." *Outside Magazine*, August 29, 2021. https://www.outsideonline.com/health/wellness/why-type-two-fun-feels-so-good/.

Louv, Richard. *Last Child in the Woods: Saving Our Children from Nature-Deficit Disorder*. Algonquin, 2005.

Munson, Richard. *Tesla: Inventor of the Modern*. Norton, 2018.

Murie, Adolph. *The Wolves of Mount McKinley*. 1944. Reprint, University of Washington Press, 1985.

Naiman, Rubin R. *Healing Night: The Science and Spirit of Sleeping, Dreaming, and Awakening*. 2nd ed. CreateSpace, 2016.

Nash, Roderick Frazier. *Wilderness and the American Mind*. 5th ed. Yale University Press, 2014.

"Nation to Be Dark One Minute Tonight After Edison Burial." *The New York Times*, October 21, 1931, 1.

National Park Service. "Nature & Science." Isle Royale National Park. https://www.nps.gov/isro/learn/nature/index.htm.

———. "Park Statistics." Isle Royale National Park. https://www.nps.gov/isro/learn/management/statistics.htm.

Nero, Robert W. *Redwings*. Smithsonian Institution Press, 1984.

Nice, Margaret Morse. *Research Is a Passion with Me: The Autobiography of Margaret Morse Nice*. Consolidated Amethyst, 1979.

———. *Studies in the Life History of the Song Sparrow, Vol. 1: A Population Study of the Song Sparrow*. 1937. Reprint, Dover, 1964.

———. *Studies in the Life History of the Song Sparrow, Vol. 2: The Behavior of the Song Sparrow and Other Passerines*. 1943. Reprint, Dover, 1964.

———. *The Watcher at the Nest*. 1939. Reprint, Dover, 1967,

Orwell, George. *Nineteen Eighty-Four*. 1949. Reprint, Berkley, 2003.

Pastor, John. *What Should a Clever Moose Eat? Natural History, Ecology, and the North Woods*. Island Press, 2016.

Perkins, Cyndi. "What Studying Moose Bones for 65 Years Can Teach Us About Human Diseases." *Unscripted Research Blog*, Michigan Technological University, January 16, 2024. https://www.mtu.edu/unscripted/2024/01/what-studying-moose-bones-for-65-years-can-teach-us-about-human-diseases.html.

Perlman, Jim, Ed Folsom, and Dan Campion. *Walt Whitman: The Measure of His Song, 200th Birthday Edition*. Holy Cow! Press, 2019.

Peterson, Carolyn C. *A View from the Wolf's Eye*. Isle Royale Natural History Association, 2008.

Peterson, Rolf O. *The Wolves of Isle Royale: A Broken Balance*. University of Michigan Press, 2007.

Reiss, Benjamin. *Wild Nights: How Taming Sleep Created Our Restless World*. Basic, 2017.

Romanski, Mark C., Elizabeth K. Orning, Kenneth F. Kellner, et al. *Wolves and the Isle Royale Environment: Restoring an Island Ecosystem, 2018-2020*. National Park Service, Isle Royale National Park, 2020.

Root, Robert, and Jill Burkland. *The Island Within Us: Isle Royale Artists in Residence 1991-1998*. Isle Royale Natural History Association, 2000.

Rucker, Mike. "Type II Fun: Embracing Hard Fun for Personal Growth." *Psychology Today*, April 30, 2024. https://www.psychologytoday.com/us/blog/the-science-of-fun/202404/type-ii-fun-embracing-hard-fun-for-personal-growth.

Samet, Matt. *Climbing Dictionary: Mountaineering Slang, Terms, Neologisms and Lingo*. Mountaineers, 2011.

Scott, Rebecca, Julien Cayla, and Bernard Cova. "Selling Pain to the Saturated Self." *Journal of Consumer Research* 44 (2017): 22–43.

Sendak, Maurice. *In the Night Kitchen*. 1970. Reprint, HarperCollins, 2023.

———. *Outside Over There*. HarperCollins, 1981.

———. *Where the Wild Things Are*. 1963. Reprint, HarperCollins, 2012.

Sharkey, Joe. "Helping the Stars Take Back the Night." *The New York Times*, August 30, 2008.

Simpson, Sherry. *Dominion of Bears: Living with Wildlife in Alaska*. University Press of Kansas, 2013.

———. "A Man Made Cold by the Universe." In *Alaska Reader: Voices from the North*, edited by Anne Hanley and Carolyn Kremers, 49–60. Chicago Review Press, 2005.

Stone, Philip R. "Making Absent Death Present: Consuming Dark Tourism in Contemporary Society." In *The Darker Side of Travel: The Theory and Practice of Dark Tourism*, edited by Richard Sharpley and Philip R. Stone, 23–38. Channel View, 2009.

Strong, Paul. *Call of the Loon*. NorthWord Press, 1995.

"Tesla: Life and Legacy." PBS. https://www.pbs.org/tesla/ll/index.html.

"Tesla Says Edison Was an Empiricist." *The New York Times*, October 19, 1931, 27.

Thoreau, Henry David. *A Week on the Concord and Merrimack Rivers*. 1849. https://www.gutenberg.org/ebooks/4232.

Trachtenberg, Alan. "Whitman at Night: 'The Sleepers' in 1855." In *Leaves of Grass: The Sesquicentennial Essays*, edited by Susan Belasco, Kenneth M. Price, and Ed Folsom, 124–40. University of Nebraska Press, 2007.

Vucetich, John A. *Restoring the Balance: What Wolves Tell Us About Our Relationship with Nature.* Johns Hopkins University Press, 2021.

Walewski, Joe. *Lichens of the North Woods.* Kollath-Stensaas, 2007.

Walker, Stephen. *Beyond: The Astonishing Story of the First Human to Leave Our Planet and Journey into Space.* Harper, 2021.

Wallace, David Foster. "Consider the Lobster." *Gourmet,* August 2004, 50–64.

Whitman, Walt. "The Sleepers." In *Leaves of Grass.* The Walt Whitman Archive, edited by Matt Cohen, Ed Folsom, and Kenneth M. Price.

———. "So Long!" In *Leaves of Grass.* The Walt Whitman Archive, edited by Matt Cohen, Ed Folsom, and Kenneth M. Price.

———. "Song of Myself." In *Leaves of Grass.* The Walt Whitman Archive, edited by Matt Cohen, Ed Folsom, and Kenneth M. Price.

Wildt, Tanya. "Michigan's Isle Royale Is One of the Least Visited National Parks in America." *Detroit Free Press,* February 29, 2024.

Woolf, Virginia. "Moments of Being." *The New York Times,* November 14, 1976.

———. *A Room of One's Own.* 1929. Reprint, Harvest, 1989.

———. *To the Lighthouse.* 1927. Reprint, Norton, 2023.

———. "Women and Fiction." In *Virginia Woolf: Collected Essays, Vol. 2,* 141–48. Harcourt, Brace & World, 1967.

"Word of the Year 2023." *Merriam-Webster,* November 27, 2023.

Yake, Bill. "Half the Forest Is Night." *Terrain.org,* November 15, 2016.

Yong, Ed. *An Immense World: How Animal Senses Reveal the Hidden Realms Around Us.* Random House, 2023.

Yoon, Carol Kaesuk. "Getting the Feel of a Long Ago Arms Race." *The New York Times,* February 7, 1995.

"Yuri Gagarin: Sixty Years Since the First Man Went into Space." *BBC,* April 11, 2021.

Zamyatin, Yevgeny. *We.* Translated by Mirra Ginsburg. Avon, 1987.

Zweig, Paul. *Walt Whitman: The Making of the Poet.* Basic, 1984.

CRUX, THE GEORGIA SERIES IN LITERARY NONFICTION

Debra Monroe, *My Unsentimental Education*
Sonja Livingston, *Ladies Night at the Dreamland*
Jericho Parms, *Lost Wax: Essays*
Priscilla Long, *Fire and Stone: Where Do We Come From? What Are We? Where Are We Going?*
Sarah Gorham, *Alpine Apprentice*
Tracy Daugherty, *Let Us Build Us a City*
Brian Doyle, *Hoop: A Basketball Life in Ninety-Five Essays*
Michael Martone, *Brooding: Arias, Choruses, Lullabies, Follies, Dirges, and a Duet*
Andrew Menard, *Learning from Thoreau*
Dustin Parsons, *Exploded View: Essays on Fatherhood, with Diagrams*
Clinton Crockett Peters, *Pandora's Garden: Kudzu, Cockroaches, and Other Misfits of Ecology*
André Joseph Gallant, *A High Low Tide: The Revival of a Southern Oyster*
Justin Gardiner, *Beneath the Shadow: Legacy and Longing in the Antarctic*
Emily Arnason Casey, *Made Holy: Essays*
Sejal Shah, *This Is One Way to Dance: Essays*
Lee Gutkind, *My Last Eight Thousand Days: An American Male in His Seventies*
Cecile Pineda, *Entry without Inspection: A Writer's Life in El Norte*
Anjali Enjeti, *Southbound: Essays on Identity, Inheritance, and Social Change*
Clinton Crockett Peters, *Mountain Madness: Found and Lost in the Peaks of America and Japan*
Steve Majors, *High Yella: A Modern Family Memoir*
Julia Ridley Smith, *The Sum of Trifles*
Siân Griffiths, *The Sum of Her Parts: Essays*
Ned Stuckey-French, *One by One, the Stars: Essays*
John Griswold, *The Age of Clear Profit: Collected Essays on Home and the Narrow Road*
Debra Monroe, *It Takes a Worried Woman: Essays*
Joseph Geha, *Kitchen Arabic: How My Family Came to America and the Recipes We Brought with Us*
Lawrence Lenhart, *Backvalley Ferrets: A Rewilding of the Colorado Plateau*
Sarah Beth Childers, *Prodigals: A Sister's Memoir of Appalachia*
Jodi Varon, *Your Eyes Will Be My Window: Essays*
Sandra Gail Lambert, *My Withered Legs and Other Essays*
Brooke Champagne, *Nola Face: Memoirs of a Truth-Telling Latina in the Big Easy*
Maddie Norris, *The Wet Wound: An Elegy in Essays*
Cris Mazza, *The Decade of Letting Things Go: A Postmenopause Memoir*
Lydia Paar, *The Exit Is the Entrance: Essays on Escape*
Joe Bonomo, *Play This Book Loud: Noisy Essays*
Wes Jamison, *My Corpse Inside*
Ashley Anderson, *Sifting the Feminine: Essays on a Woman's Body*